THE NAME OF GOD IS LOVE

First published in 2022 by
New Life Publishing, Luton,
Bedfordshire LU3 4DQ

© Chris Thomas

British Library Cataloguing in Publication Data
A catalogue record for this book is available
from the British Library

ISBN 978 1 912237 41 8

Unless otherwise stated Bible references are
from the New Jerusalem Bible Readers Edition,
first published 1985 by Darton Longman
& Todd Limited and Doubleday and Co., Inc.,
and used with permission.

Typesetting by New Life Publishing,
Luton, UK www.goodnewsbooks.co.uk
Printed and bound in Great Britain

THE NAME OF GOD

IS LOVE

Chris Thomas

CONTENTS

INTRODUCTION

M Y FRIEND MAUREEN WAS TELLING ME ONE DAY THAT WHILE she believed God loved her, she found it exceedingly difficult to read the Old or First Testament. This was because she thought the God of ancient Israel she encountered was vastly different from the God she knew and had experienced in her life. She also spoke of hell and purgatory which she said did nothing to help in her journey into love. Maureen is a woman of faith and is prepared to struggle with this issue, but I can understand why, for many people, what stumbling blocks for faith these things are.

Can a loving God will the widespread destruction of people? Can a compassionate, caring God smite the enemies of God's people or wreak vengeance on those who fail to keep God's will? Can a God who is love send people to hell and purgatory with all the imagery we have been given of those places? Sadly, many of us in our guts at a deep, almost unconscious level, think that God does precisely that. When bad things are happening, God does not love us anymore and we will be punished for all eternity; we are being punished for what we have done wrong. What does that say about our image of God? That God is vengeful and angry?

I do not believe that such a God exists, and it is certainly not the image of God that Jesus has. His image of God is a God of love, tenderness and goodness, the God of the prodigal son and the shepherd who goes out looking for the sheep. The God Jesus revealed is a God of love. It is when we get off the roundabout of trying to earn God's love that we fall in love with God; then we can do nothing else but love the Lord our God with everything that we are.

We were created to dance. We were made to be filled with awe and wonder at goodness. Somehow, we have to trust that and believe it. It is right at the core of our belief. It is at the heart of what Jesus was about. He turned on its head the narrow judgemental image of God that the scribes and Pharisees taught and invited us into a broad, spacious understanding of who God is. The challenge is to open ourselves to the love that is in the heart of the father for us. There is no need to be afraid.

So can we get over the problems that face so many of us? I think reading the scriptures with the aid of contemporary scripture study, we can. I am also sure that by re-visiting doctrines with current theology, we can let go of images of God which are largely unhelpful. We can begin to see the truth that God takes us as we are and leads us gently towards the full revelation of who God is in Jesus.

This book in its faltering way is for all those who struggle with images of God that seem contradictory. It is for those who are journeying in faith and want to let go of things they carry with them about God. It is for those setting out to discover the God of Jesus and the wonderful life we are called to.

ONE

AN ENCOUNTER WITH LOVE

L IVERPOOL IN THE 1960's WAS AN EXCITING PLACE TO BE, BUT IT was also a place of great poverty and struggle. I suppose my early life could be summed up in those two words. We were poor, living in the upstairs of a semi-detached house and sharing the toilet with the patients of a doctor's surgery housed below; and we struggled. We were poor because my dad was alcoholic and as a result of that we struggled to hold things together as a family, despite my mum's best efforts.

My Dad was about 52 when I was born. He was brought up in a lower middle-class home in Edwardian England. Dad was the youngest of four brothers, the eldest of whom, Desmond, had died in the First World War. After that war, my grandmother wrote to Queen Mary and told her that she would never be able to afford to go to Italy where Des was buried after being shot down in 1918. She asked the Queen, who was about to embark on a tour of war graves, if she could get the official photographer to take a picture of his grave. Some months later a package arrived with the said pictures. The Queen had responded to a mother's need. However Desmond's death played its part in my dad's background. His father became hard and cynical and did not really treat his other three sons very well; and his mother was never physically well until her death in 1943 at the relatively young age of 68.

I am told that Dad played tennis and danced and laughed during the Twenties and was always the centre of attention at parties. He had passed the 11 Plus and gone to grammar school, but left at the age of 14 and joined the merchant navy which he loved. The Second World War was pivotal in his life. The Omaha beach landings, Dunkirk, and seeing many of his friend die around him changed him, and he returned home a different man, much more like his father than he ever cared to admit. I finally understood what it must have been like for him during the war when I saw the film, 'Saving Private Ryan' which began with the Beach landings. I sobbed as I realised something of his pain. When he returned to England, he found his mother had died, his father had given up the family home and gone to live with one of his sisters, and there were few jobs to be found. Dad was a real casualty of war. He found a room in his aunt Florrie's house and set about looking for a job. He became an insurance agent for a while, the first in a long line of dead-end jobs. It was while living with Florrie and her husband Pat, that he met my mum, Vera French, at a dance in St Hugh's church hall in Liverpool. She was 24 and he was 39. Mum was shy, gentle and beautiful and he was quickly besotted. She had just broken up with a long-term boyfriend and my grandmother told that her she had better grab this chance with my dad while she could, or she would be 'left on the shelf.' They married on December 27th 1947. I came along thirteen years later, the youngest of five, three of whom had died. The deaths of the three older children certainly had their effect. Mum could never speak of them, and dad retreated into himself and the bottle as a means of escape.

Mum and dad's relationship was turbulent to say the least. Dad seemed to have no drive within him and would settle for the least while mum, despite her gentleness, wanted so much more from life. She wanted to own a house, which she never did because dad would not entertain it. She wanted to become a teacher, but dad thought that would take her away from the family and so it was not even considered. It was made all the harder because my aunty Maureen qualified as a teacher as a mature student. Mum's brother, Bob, taught her to drive because dad could not perceive of his wife driving a car, any more than he wanted her to go to work, which of course she did off her own volition. I remember screaming fights as a child which terrified me, and which would reduce my mum to a wreck, but she could never give up. It was a fight for her life.

Dad never called me by name or played with me as a child. I was always 'boy'. The closest I ever got to him was when I would go with him to the off licence and carry back his bottles of Scotsmac, a rough blend of whisky and wine. Never physically violent, but certainly emotionally abusive, Dad could lose his temper in a second and I lived with a high level of anxiety because I never knew what he would do. This anxiety led to physical sickness, and I was often referred to the hospital, only for mum to be told I was a nervous child. We all knew that, and why! When I was very young, Dad would often pack a suitcase and leave, only to return after a few hours, or sometimes days. His tempers could last for weeks, and we would all creep around the flat trying not to antagonise him.

I am a very sensitive person and I love animals and flowers and music. I told stories and read books and cried in the cinema. My Dad's experience was that the world was a hard place, and I guess he felt I wouldn't survive; and so he seemed to have a crusade against my sensitivity. Everything that was sensitive and artistic within me was laughed at or ignored. Pets were treated cruelly and sometimes just got rid of. Snowy, a white Alsatian who sensed my anxiety and fear of the dark, would come with me to bed. Each night there would be a fight between my dad and the dog as dad tried to drag him out of the room saying that I had to learn to be strong. I came home from school one day to find that Snowy had gone. It was years later that mum told me that dad had him destroyed. I remember one day coming home to a flat we lived in at the time and finding my pet rabbit dead in the yard. Dad had broken its neck because it had bitten him. Books were ripped up, instruments got rid of and my tears laughed at. All of this led to more rows between mum and dad about how to bring children up and I would quake in my bedroom, shaking and crying silently, thinking it was all my fault.

I wanted my dad to love me but, as a child, I never experienced that love. I am sure now that my dad did love me. I just think he was a broken man who was unable to deal with his own pain; and I think it is true that what you are unable to process, you pass on to others.

That's why it is vital that we confront our inner demons and learn the lessons they teach us. It is of immense importance that we face ourselves and let go of the dross we carry so that we can begin to know what humanity is about. If we do not touch our brokenness, we simply pass it on to those around us, to our wives or husbands, to our children; and another generation learns to blame rather than acknowledge, accept and love.

So do allow yourself to face your own pain and vulnerability and know the truth that God will be there. Tell your stories to one another and let go. Recognise the God who is with you. Open your eyes and see yourself as God sees you without your masks, in all your fragility and vulnerability as the most precious child there is. I really do believe that only by facing all the hurts and pain in life will we come to that realisation and find life in it. That knowledge of being loved will help you accept things about yourself that you would rather reject. Sometimes we will need the power of healing. Sometimes we will need the sacrament of reconciliation. The Spirit will enable us to find the peace that our hearts desire.

Take responsibility for your inner life and allow the Spirit to lead you through it. Learn the process of letting go so that when we have to let go of this stage of life itself, it will only be another stage on the journey. It is only by doing that and being compassionate and loving with yourself that you will be able to be compassionate and loving with those you love. It is only by learning not to judge yourself that you'll learn not to judge others. It is only by learning to forgive yourself that you will learn to forgive others. If the world learnt that lesson, can you imagine how much happier things would be?

So, back to my childhood. It was difficult, but not bad all the time. Mum was kind and loved us very much, always putting my brother and me before herself. I remember lots of days out and hard-won holidays in local seaside resorts. We would stay in cheap boarding houses and go out every day with dad trailing behind us, usually with a hip flask secreted upon his person and a sour look on his face.

I loved Christmas time because Christmas day was the only day when we did not have to tiptoe around Dad. He always seemed in a good mood, even when he was too drunk to stand up from his chair. Boxing day was a different story as he struggled with the effects of alcohol! So, my childhood Christmases are filled with good memories. I remember going to bed each Christmas Eve with the house as normal and then, because of the excitement, waking up early on Christmas morning and finding myself in the middle of fairyland with the Christmas tree and lights and decorations everywhere. Mum and dad worked for hours to get the house ready, making sure not to wake us up. When I was four, I had sent a letter to Santa telling him that I wanted Lenny the lion for Christmas. Lenny was a popular stuffed toy with a smiling face and real whiskers, or so I thought! I woke up on Christmas morning to find Lenny sitting in the pillowcase along with a selection box, a tangerine and an apple. I was so excited that I burst out crying and Nana, who lived with us and, like my mum, was kindness itself, came into our room. I remember hugging her and Lenny at the same time and stammering out, 'Look Nana…Lenny came, Lenny came.' I still remember her laughing and then saying to me, 'just remember that as much as you love Lenny and wanted Lenny, God loves you; and Christmas time is all about God showing us that we are loved.' She then said to me as long as you have Lenny, I want you to look at him and remember what Christmas is about. I still have Lenny 58 years later and I look at him every Christmas morning and remember.

So it was not all bad, but those early childhood experiences scarred me extremely badly. By the time I was fifteen I was sullen and angry. I had built barriers around my heart to protect myself and even though the rows had ended by then, my relationship with dad was inextricably damaged. I was a mass of contradictions and insecurities, and no one seemed to notice. The only thing I was sure about was that I did not want to live my life as Dad had lived his. I passed the 11 Plus and went to grammar school, although that was not really a good experience. It was a tough regime, as it was in those days, with lots of violence, and so I was anxious at school as well as at home although nobody knew. I am reasonably intelligent and articulate and I wanted to pass my exams and get out of Liverpool, as far away as possible. My brother Paul did exactly that, joining the merchant navy as dad had done. He had a brief time back in Liverpool where he got a degree and then went to Newcastle where he got a doctorate. Eventually having lived all over the world, he settled in the Philippines, a place he loved very much. I used to dream of living abroad and creating a new persona for myself. I appeared cold, hard and uncommunicative, yet deep inside I ached to be loved but was frightened to let anyone love me. Then I encountered God when I was 15.

I still love football, but then I was a fanatical Liverpool fan. I
guess it was the one place where I could lose myself and not
feel as though I did not measure up. Five days before my 16th
birthday Liverpool's home game with, I think, Birmingham City
was cancelled, and I was angry. Dad was off work and would
probably drink himself into a stupor; mum was going out and
all I had to look forward to was hanging around the shops in the
city centre. My mum, without telling me what I was going to,
asked me to go out with her and the miracle was that I went. I
had not been in the habit of going out with mum for a long time.

We picked up a couple of 'crazies' on the way who kept talking
about Jesus and saying 'Praise the Lord' every few minutes.
Unbeknown to me, my mum had been attending a prayer group
for a couple of years each Friday night and I was being taken to
a day of charismatic renewal. It was like a parallel universe. This
was the mid-seventies when renewal was sweeping around the
world and the spirit of God was transforming lives, turning
people upside down and setting people free. We arrived at a
church hall in Warrington where some four hundred people had
gathered. As we were a little late things had already got under-
way. People were clapping and dancing and singing. I wanted
to get out. I thought everyone around me was mad, but I was
not able to leave because my mum was next to me, and I could
not get out of the bench, and where would I go anyway? I was
miles from home without any money. Eventually the praise
stopped and a man, I later discovered he was a priest called Jim
Brandt, got up and began to talk about Jesus. He interspersed
his talk with bits of classical music played on a grand piano and

I can only say I heard him deeply within myself. He talked of Jesus' love, his relationship with God's people and the power of God. He told stories of how people had experienced Jesus in their lives, and I knew that I wanted to know Jesus the way he did.

If you have never had the experience of coming alive in God, then search for it and want it with all your heart. I was standing in that hall in Warrington at the beginning of 1976 with a desire in my heart to know Jesus. Suddenly I was filled with a red-hot flush of pins and needles and then I began to weep. It was an experience that lasted about ten minutes. Those around me began to lay hands on me. I tried to shrug them off but, in the end, gave in and allowed them to lay hands on me. Unintelligible sounds came out of my mouth. I did wonder at one point if I was having a stroke. When the pins and needles finally dissipated, I was left with one truth - that I was loved by God. More than that God was in love with me. That truth changed my life.

Since that experience which I have reflected on many times, it seems to me that our role as church is to try to enable people to discover in a real and experiential way that God exists, that God is alive, and that, because of this, there is a purpose to our own lives and a love that is deeper than anything we can ever imagine, a love within which we are held and cherished beyond our wildest imaginings. Ronald Rolheiser, the well known author and speaker says that, 'our first task in ministry is to tell people that they are being held, unconditionally and inescapably, in the hands of a living and loving God and that this God is delighting in them.' God delights in you and me. It is the most extraordinary truth that changed my life and enabled me, in time, to let go of my hurt and find deep inner healing, a process that is not finished yet. I guess because of that powerful unconditional love, I have realised that there is a deep goodness to be found in the Universe and within me and every human person who lives. Search for goodness, look for love and compassion. It is all around us.

I think I began to realise that the truth of love, and the goodness that lies at the heart of everything, is far more important than dogma or doctrine or denominational boundaries It is more important and more invigorating than moral codes, liturgy authority structures and about right or wrong. It is of far more value for people to realise that they are unconditionally loved by God and held by the source and origin of all life. Everything else will follow in time.

After my experience I thought I had arrived. One of the discoveries I have made on my journey is that if you bury things from your past, they have a way of biting back. With the discovery of earth-shattering love, my journey had only just started. My life had been completely turned upside down at that event and I knew that I wanted to live for the Gospel and nothing else. I joined a prayer group, and my life became an endless round of events and experiences, which is both good and bad for us. I met amazing people who became life long friends. Life was good and God was good. I eventually trained to be a catholic priest and was ordained by Archbishop Worlock in 1985.

However, I never dealt with the pain and insecurity of my childhood. I lurched around in a low-level depression for years, always feeling bad because I had met Jesus and yet was never really at peace. I was a Priest and should not feel this way. I eventually went into a deep depression that nothing would make go away and I had to go for help.

It was during the sessions with a counsellor who became my 'God with skin on', and because of the prayer that I was soaked in during that time that I emerged like a butterfly from its cocoon, and I began to rejoice in being me. I guess that is where I am up to now.

I still have my moments of insecurity and fear which come from a place deep within, but I am learning how to face them and work through them. I believe that every day is gift, and even the days when I feel fragile and unsure remind me of how much I need God.

So much of the spiritual journey has to do with dealing with the inner life and facing our emotions and working through them and little to do with doing religious things. I thank God every day for all that has been because, without the experiences I have had, I would not be me and I thank God for all that is; and I look forward to all that will be, knowing the truth that God is with me.

That experience of knowing the unconditional love of God changed my life and its trajectory. One of the gifts I was given at that time, which has never left me, was a real thirst for the Word of God. I loved the Bible and the way it revealed the face of God to me. It was the word that helped me over years to both root and affirm the truth of unconditional love in my psyche. I was not filled with joy during my time in the seminary. Much of the teaching we received, and the liturgy we celebrated, seemed alien to me as did my experience of God to many of the other students and staff. I was, however, delighted to be able to spend time studying the scriptures, absorbing them and allowing them to take on new depth and meaning. I was opened up to wisdom far beyond anything I would have been able to find by myself. I was taught, mainly, by men who loved the scriptures and who approached them in both an academic way and a pastoral way. Like me, they loved the Word of God, and I sat at their feet and drank in the wonders they shared with me. Their scholarship enabled me to move away from a narrow fundamentalist approach to the scriptures to something that was far broader and more spacious. Richard Rohr, the American Franciscan writes, 'Fundamentalism refuses to listen to the deep levels of mythic, metaphorical, and mystical meaning. It is obsessed with literalism and exclusion. The egoic need for clarity and certitude leads fundamentalists to use sacred writings in a mechanical, closed-ended, and quite authoritarian manner.' The more I read the scriptures with a new set of eyes, the more I realised that what I had experienced was true; that God is pure unconditional love. We human beings are not condemned but loved and God is calling us to let go of our certitudes and let God reveal Godself to us in a new, radical and dynamic way which, yes, turns us upside down but which brings vibrant, fulfilled life.

I have been told that Franciscan theology teaches that love always comes before knowledge. It seems that we human beings can only know that which we love. Without that experience of love we will distort the knowledge we have to build up our ego. We have to let go and fall into grace if we are to grow and change and open ourselves to the revelation of love. Grace is never something we deserve but something we fall into. We do not receive more grace for living a good and righteous life, for being moral or religious. It is something we are immersed into when we open up to love. The Scriptures tell the story of a people who just do not get it. In both the First and Second Testaments we are told of the inability of people to open up to a new vision of God. We find in the Second Testament, Jesus telling the parable of the generous landowner and the vineyard workers who are all invited to work in the vineyard for different periods of time and who all receive the same reward. This is the wonder of grace, but sadly we do not get it, and want to earn it or be rewarded by it rather than fall into it. All that we do is to create God in our own image and likeness and God becomes punitive and small-minded rather than gracious and loving. When God is made in our image and likeness, all human and spiritual growth comes to an end and we become defensive and narrow, and it kills us within because we can never fall into grace.

What I will try to do in this book is to let the Scriptures speak to us of who God really is, to see in their revelation the truth of love and the intimacy that God desires with us. I hope that wherever we are in our journey in faith, we would have the courage to let go and open up to the experience of love that shatters us and causes to rebuild who we think we are, again and again and again.

TWO

GOD IS NOT AN ANGRY GOD

MANY YEARS AGO, I WAS AT A CONFERENCE LEADING A workshop entitled 'God is not angry'. There were about fifty people there and we were trying to explore why there seems to be a God in the First or Old Testament who is vengeful and angry and who destroys the enemies of God's people. Then in the Second or New Testament, God seems to have changed into a loving caring God. It's an image which seems to be in direct contrast to the other image of God and it can make us very confused as we try to relate to God. We believe in a God who is unconditionally loving and yet might just be into 'pay back' time. As I am sure you can see, the two do not go together.

The question that seemed to be hovering around as the group were sharing was, 'how can we trust God when God, in the Bible, seems to change so easily from angry and vengeful to loving and compassionate? So we were reflecting on that as a group. I had made several points during the conversation about cultural realities and perceptions which I hope to address during this chapter. It seemed to go quite well and several people said they felt quite stretched and challenged during the session. We came to the end and one woman remained behind. I was tidying up when I realised she was still there and that she was crying. I sat down next to her, and the crying got worse. When she finally calmed down, she told me that she had spent most of her life being frightened of God. As a young girl, she had been brought up in a very small, extremely insular, brethren church where a God of fear and damnation had been preached. As a result of her upbringing, she had grown up with an image of God that terrified her. After she became a Catholic during her time at university, she was never away from the confessional because she always felt guilty and worthy only of punishment. For what, she could never really say. However, if anyone had asked her the question 'does God love you?', her answer would have been an irrevocable yes. She had been fed an image of a mean-spirited, narrow-minded God who, yes, loved her but only if she acted within certain parameters! What a tension to live with.

As she sat listening in our workshop, her whole image of God began to crumble. She realised we do not have a pay-back God, and that the moral structure on which she had built her life owed more to the small minded adults that she had met on her journey than it had to do with God. She began to see that the God of the First Testament and the God of the Second Testament were exactly the same and that God's name was, and always had been, love. She sobbed with relief as she realised that there was no need to be afraid.

Many of us have lived our lives afraid of God, anxious in case some petty misdemeanor, particularly in the area of sexuality, should send us plunging into the fires of hell for all eternity. What sort of God would do that to us, the pinnacle of creation? Fear of God never brings peace but simply perpetuates the idea that God is vengeful and angry. However, our God is a God of endless patient love and I believe that can be borne out by any patient reading of the scriptures with a good commentary in front of us.

I think it is true that if you read some of the stories in the First Testament at a fundamentalist level, you would find a disturbing image of God. The ancient writers tell stories of battles and wars where God is perceived as being on the side of the people of Israel and almost wills destruction and warfare.

I love watching Louis Theroux documentaries on television. He has spent a lot of time in America's bible belt with some 'supposed' Christians who see God as being on the far right of American politics. There have been various programmes down the years where Louis has interviewed people who actively promoted a God who wanted to destroy those who were not fulfilling God's will as they interpreted it.

They were using a literal interpretation of the First Testament to justify an image of God that is far removed from the image presented by Jesus. To illustrate the point, I would like to reflect on the book of Joshua where the Israelites, having crossed the Red Sea, took the land of Canaan. The way in which they conquered Canaan was by defeating local armies, killing survivors, and burning their cities. If you take that literally, then the image of God it presents us with is horrendous. However, as I try to show below, this way of acting was better than a more primitive morality in which conquered people were tortured, their women and children raped and enslaved, and their possessions looted.

In the story the Israelites were told to place the cities under a ban, which meant to consecrate it and set it apart for the Lord. They were not allowed to put the people into slavery nor were they to use the people's possessions for their own good. The town was to be destroyed and offered to the Lord. It is a good example of how God always meets people where they are and calls them forward one step at a time. There is an old adage, 'God loves me as I am but too much to leave me there.' God did not ask the people of Israel to abide by the just war theory or by principles of non-violence which were alien to all peoples of the day. The people of God believed that God had told them to take the city of Jericho and destroy everything in it but to take nothing for themselves.

They were to offer everything to God so that in time, they would come to see that they could not depend on this way of life for happiness. It was a slow evolutionary growth in morality. It was not a full revelation of who God is. How can we believe in a God of compassion and mercy and love when that same God seems to advocate this sort of warfare? I think the truth is that God, who is unchanging, would never will the destruction of innocent people, but it seems as though it were God's will that the people of Israel possess the land. Because the people were conditioned by the prevailing practices of the day, they could never perceive of any other way. So, they took land with brutality and with violence. Then they wrote down the story in a way that makes it appear as though God told them how to do it. I think the truth is that God can bring good out of the strangest circumstances, even, at times, situations of great evil; but it was not God's will that the people were destroyed. That was all about human perceptions and understanding and moral development.

If you go to the Second Testament you find a God who is revealed as the father of Jesus - loving, compassionate, forgiving and merciful. You find a God who, in Jesus, heals the poor and the broken. In Jesus' manifesto in Luke chapter 4, we hear, Jesus using the words of the prophet Isaiah, that he came to set prisoners free, bring sight to the blind and proclaim the Lord's year of favour. It is all about transformation, new life, new possibility as love is poured out upon the world. I often look at the scriptures and wonder what it must have been like to be one of those who encountered Jesus and the loving God he revealed. What was it like for the feisty Samaritan woman who had to let her barriers down? What about the woman who was found in the act of committing adultery and came face to face with mercy and compassion? What must it have been like to be Peter's mother-in-law or the man born blind or the woman who had been bleeding for years? They all knew the reality of God's amazing love for them because of Jesus. What about little Zaccheus, who climbed a sycamore tree to get sight of Jesus and got a whole lot more than he bargained for. How about the rich young man who walks away but who is loved anyway? Every word of the Gospels tells of an extraordinary love. In typically rabbinic style, Jesus' parables and stories speak of a God of passionate love; the Prodigal son, the story of the shepherd who leaves his sheep and goes out searching for the one that is lost, the landowner who pays all his workers the same wage regardless of the hours worked. The stories go on and on. In fact,

Jesus' harshest words are reserved for those who refuse to acknowledge the love of God for all people. He berates those who cannot, because of tradition and narrow interpretation of the law, allow God to break through. I often think, is it any wonder that the tax collectors and the supposed sinners were beating a path to Jesus? His image of God brought life. He preached, through word and action, a God who can cope with mess and with mistakes. Jesus told those who came to him - and tells us - about a God who loves all humanity; but more than that about a God who can only love us both individually and collectively. This was in direct contrast to the prevailing image of God that the scribes and the Pharisees peddled, an image that did not bring life but stultifying inner death. It is no wonder that they flocked to Jesus.

That dichotomy between the God of the First Testament and the God of the Second means that lots of people read the Second Testament because it is more palatable than the First Testament, and seemingly more easily understood. Yet, to do that deprives us of a wealth of beauty and understanding that could be ours.

So, does God change between the First and Second Testament? I think the answer is no. It is the same God who is constantly revealing Godself to us. That revelation is one of loving faithfulness and compassion, ultimately made flesh in Jesus. It is then we can see and understand the revelation of God. I think what happens is that the people of God grow and change and develop. Is that not what we are always doing, changing and developing, and is it not true that God always meet us where we are?

I think part of the problem lies in the way we understand inspiration. As I have already made clear, many people treat the Bible in a narrow fundamentalist way, believing that the words used simply dropped out of heaven. In his wonderful book, 'Great Themes of Scripture', Richard Rohr addresses the problem when he writes, 'Fundamentalism is a slavish idealisation of words which inevitably leads to a rigid closed minded dead ended approach to the Bible.'

Within the Catholic tradition, that is not what we believe about the inspired Word of God. The books of the Bible are not meant to be taken literally. What we hold to be true is that the Scriptures contain all that is necessary for life. The Bible tells us the truth of who God is and the truth of who we are. It issues an invitation to be in relationship with God, with our brothers and sisters and with every created reality. It reminds us of the truth about our destiny and the call to be in union with God now and forever. In order to really understand what this bible is about, we have to look for the religious truth that lies behind the words.

Just for a moment, I would like to go back to the example from the book of Joshua and the story of the destruction of Jericho. What the ancient writers were trying to tell us was that the people of Israel were to devote themselves completely to God and to nothing else; that God would be their strength, that God would be their provider. That is religious truth. That is the inspired level of the word of God. It is not the same as historical accuracy or scientific explanation. The religious truth that the Bible tells us is of a God who is unconditionally loving, constantly reaching out to humanity with a passionate intensity that we find so difficult to deal with. All of which is eventually captured in the person of Jesus.

In inspiring the Bible, God worked through human beings who had the cultural and intellectual limitations of their day. As I have already shared, they believed in warfare and violence as a way of life. They wrote in ancient languages that we cannot interpret very clearly, and they had customs and practices and ways of thinking that were very different to ours. The authors used literary forms to meet the needs of their audiences. There are ancient myths and legends, poems, letters, songs, genealogies, laws, accounts of visions, and stories passed from generation to generation.

The important questions to ask when reading the Scriptures are, 'What is it saying to us about life? What is it saying to us about love? What is it saying about reality? How is it leading me deeply into the mystery that is God? What am I discovering about myself and about my value and worth?'

So, who is the God revealed to us in the Scriptures? From the beginning to the end, the Scriptures tell us that God is extra-ordinary, amazing love. God is always trying to touch our lives that we might be drawn more fully into the mystery that is love. I have written this before, but someone once said to me that the Bible is a love story between God and God's people, and like any love story it has its ups and downs but ultimately it is about love which is completely poured out and the reaction to that love. At the heart of the collection of books we call the Bible is a God who deliberately and purposefully allows the outrageous, irresistible power of love to flow into the world.

One of the greatest influences in my life is an Irish woman called Frances Hogan. I met her after the experience I described in the previous chapter. Frances has long been a wonderful exponent of the scriptures and has travelled all over the world breaking open the word of God. It was she who awoke within me a love of the bible, and it was she who showed me that the God of the First and Second Testament has the same name, and that name is love.

So now I would like to try and take a mad dash through the Scriptures and see how they reveal this God of love. The book of Genesis beautifully remembers that God creates out of love. Every aspect of creation reveals the dynamic wonder of creative love. The universe, the world, every living creature, is a result of love gushing out and taking shape and form. When reflecting on the creation of human beings, it is wonderful to know that each of us was wanted whatever the circumstance of our birth, by a God whose love is at the very core of our being. The books of Deuteronomy and Exodus show the forming of a nation bound together by a God who loves and frees us. Throughout what are called the historical books and on into the prophets, you discover if you have eyes that see, a God who is desperately in love with us. That God meets us where we are, gently leading us towards the full revelation of love in Jesus.

There are times when the people of Israel almost understand who God is, particularly in books like the beautiful Song of Songs. Some of the prophets like Hosea and his imagery of the unfaithful wife and the love that constantly takes her back, reminds us how clearly at times the prophets understood the nature of God. However, as we all know, there are times when they lose that understanding of love altogether and call down the power of God to smite their enemies. They are so like us; sometimes we glimpse the overwhelming gift of love and other times we lose it altogether.

By the time we get to the Gospels, we discover in Jesus how much we are loved by God. God reveals Godself in a human body and in a human situation. In that human body, in Jesus, we can see, touch, almost taste, God's unconditional love for us. As I said earlier, all Jesus' stories are about love, and they turn us upside down if we can only move beyond ourselves to see what he is saying. The rest of the Second Testament is a teasing out of how we understand that love. Again, these early Christian letters are sometimes tainted by culture, but at times they explode into images of love that words can barely contain. Think of Romans 8 where Paul tells us that 'nothing can separate us from the love of God' or the letter to the Ephesians where the author prays that we might know the fullness of God's love. These ancient authors, particularly Paul and his followers, will tell us repeatedly that we are not loved because of who we are, but because of who God is - immense overwhelming love. That was his experience. His road to Damascus experience is about love that meets him in the depths of his hatred and sin and turns him around to see in a different way.

I have known that turnaround in my own experience, and I have met many people whose lives have turned around because of the power of love. Jo was a young woman I met many years ago. Her face was shining with joy and her eyes sparkled with undisguised delight at the gift of life. I was teaching a course at the university alongside an Anglican priest and Jo was on the course. She was a member of a local Anglican Church and had seen the course advertised on her parish newsletter. The course was designed around people's experience of the transforming power of the Spirit and participants were given lots of opportunities to share their stories. Jo was the first to get on her feet and the honesty with which she shared was both refreshing and challenging. She told us of her early life when she was badly treated by her parents. There was some physical abuse from her father, but her mother's silence on the matter was just as hard to bear. She described how on one occasion, when she was six years old, her dad had rushed into the garden screaming at her over some perceived offence. He grabbed hold of her as she tried to escape and, in front of her friends, pulled her pants down and spanked her. Jo cried as she told us of the shame she felt as all the other children stood in silence and watched as she screamed in pain and humiliation. She went on to tell of many such occasions when her dad's anger burst out and she was usually the recipient. In school she was difficult and obviously troubled, but in the 1960's not too many questions were asked about what was happening at home She was just seen as a difficult child, and the more school complained about her behaviour, the more she was beaten at home. Her mum, too, was abused by her father, hence her silence and inability to protect her daughter down the years. It all became too much for Jo's mother and she took her own life when Jo was ten. After that tragedy, Jo continued to live in a world of violence and heartache. By the time she was fifteen Jo was pregnant and was placed in a mother and baby home. At last she was free of her father's tyranny and life in the home, austere as it was, was better than life with her father. The nuns who ran the home were, in the main, kind women who did their best. There was one sister in particular called Sister Frances, who was kindness itself and who went beyond the call of duty to make those in her charge feel that they had value and dignity despite their circumstances. This nun used to pray with the girls each night if they wanted to pray, but Jo said she always avoided the prayer. Her experiences had led her to not believe in God at all and certainly not a good God. One night when close to her time, Sr Frances asked her if she would like some prayer and Jo, terrified at the thought of giving birth said 'Yes'. She smiled as she told us that when the prayer began, she felt herself flooded with a warmth of love that turned her life around. She was no longer afraid. Life was hard for a young unmarried mother, but she knew that God was with her. She managed in time to put herself through college and became a religious teacher. She said she wanted to help others find what she had discovered, that God is love and that love is enough.

It is that love which means you are welcome in the heart of God. You have a place there. God delights in you. Whoever you are and whatever you are, you are welcome. Whatever you may have done in your life, you are welcome. Whether you are black,

white, catholic, protestant, Moslem, Hindu, believer or non-
believer, bad guy, good guy, straight or gay you have a place
in the heart of God. Philip Yancey in his book' 'What's so
Amazing About Grace' says, 'categories of worthiness do not
apply.' Wonderful words that I know in my guts to be true and
which I hope are the bedrock of my life. The desire of my heart
is that everyone should know that there is nothing you can be
and nothing you can have done, that will stop God loving you.

That is the scandal of grace; that love is freely poured out, does
not condemn and requires nothing in return. It is the reality of
who God is - unconditionally loving and compassionate. The
Bible is the most outrageous collection of books ever put
together because it slices like the finest meat cleaver through all
our attempts to be sanctimonious and respectable and worthy.
It is a love that says you are precious in the eyes of God so let go
of the need you have to control God by your good works or your
piety and simply open yourself to love.

Everywhere I go I have preached this truth and usually someone
will ask me with a smile on their face something like, 'Does that
mean I can do what I want, and God will never stop loving me?'
It is usually borne out of a desperate desire to be right with God,
but without the experience of being loved by God. When you
have been overcome by the greatest love there is, when you
know the truth of grace, you only want to do what God wants.
It is a love relationship after all. There will be mistakes made but
the motivation for your life will be about love responding to
love.

So, is the God of the Second Testament the same as the God of the First Testament. Yes! And that God is unconditionally loving and accepting and faithful. Sometimes, in order to discover that God we have to do a bit of work and reflection and prayer, but it is worth it because it will bring us life, and life in its fullness.

THREE

HELL, PURGATORY, AND LOVE

A FEW DAYS AGO I OPENED THE DOOR OF OUR SMALL RETREAT centre to find a woman that I had never met before standing there. She wanted to know the times of Mass on Sunday. I explained to her that the church was no longer a parish church but was now a centre for spirituality and outreach. She looked at me blankly and said 'what a shame.' I was about to close the door when she suddenly exploded, ranting and raving about people who no longer went to mass, which necessitated the closure of churches. 'Do they not know they are all going to hell and will burn for all eternity?' I foolishly said that I hoped they did not know that and had never been taught that and she took off again. She was angry because nobody was frightened of God or hell or purgatory anymore and that, as far as she could see, had been the undoing of the church. No wonder nobody went to church; they were not frightened enough. By this time she was screaming at me, and I did wonder if she was about to have some sort of heart attack or stroke so I offered her a cup of tea if she would like one.

She came into the house reluctantly, looking around as though she might be attacked by some sort of neo-liberals who would brainwash her into believing something about God she did not want to believe. We sat down together, and I made a pot of tea. She told me her name was Kathleen, but she would not say where she lived. It transpired that none of her children went to

31

church anymore and she thought a good dose of fear was what they needed to bring them back, as she put it, to a good religious life. Our conversation went on for about an hour and it really was quite sad. Nothing I could say could shift Kathleen from her deeply entrenched fearful stance. She quoted this saint and that visionary to support her view. I have to say I had not come across many of them. Eventually she left, a sad, bitter, unhappy woman who hoped I would change my mind in case I ended up with her children who were going to hell forever.

In this chapter before we move into the scriptures, I want to take time to look at hell and purgatory and how they sit side by side with the image of a loving God.

I am always intrigued by Christian visionaries that people seem to latch on to. Very few of them talk of love or the extraordinary nature of love. Most of them talk of souls falling into hell in their millions, with a few managing to stop in purgatory rather than completely free-falling into an eternity of torture. The first question that raises for me is whether or not such visions are the product of a healthy mind and soul. The second question is whether or not these revelations reveal a deep truth, or are they a perversion of the nature of God? I have to say I do not really think that they come from a healthy mind; nor do I think that they show us the nature of God.

It seems to me that an image of God who sends people to hell or into purgatory is not an image that we find in the scriptures unless we read them at a very fundamentalist level. However, such an image can so fill us with fear that we are concerned that every action we do might be sinful. It can lead to a sense of panic that everything we do might be sending us down the path to the fires of hell, even when we do not recognise that we might have done wrong. In turn, this can lead to scruples with the mental health issues they can bring. I do not believe that our God is concerned with sending people to hell. I remember Cardinal Cormac Murphy O'Connor once saying, 'we are duty bound to believe in hell. We are not duty bound to believe anyone is there.' Ronald Rolheiser says that, 'Hell is not full of people spending eternity regretting their mistakes on earth ... painfully wishing that they had just one minute back on earth in which to make some act of contrition which would enable them to go to heaven! I suspect that hell isn't very full at all.'

I think, like many holy people and mystics, I am a universalist which means that in the end, I believe, there is salvation for everyone and everything in the created order. At the end of time, that state of being that we call hell will be healed and transformed and all will be well. Universalists argue from a deep faith in the unconditional love of God. This love can never be overcome; it can never be defeated, and God wants everyone to experience that love for all time. My own sense of God's love is that when we meet God face to face and are overwhelmed with love, then not even the worst dictator in human history will be able to resist.

I met a man recently who spends most of his life in what he calls, 'shadowlands.' Tom believes in the power of love to transform hearts and minds and so he works with the poorest of the poor, those who live on the streets, those who live in cardboard boxes under railway bridges. He calls it the shadowlands because most 'good living' people are not aware that others live far below the poverty line, or have made choices that have wrecked their lives, or even have illnesses that have caused them to disappear from mainstream society. Where, and how, they live is the shadowlands. I was greatly impressed by this man who said that his role in the shadowlands was to bring love that illuminated the darkness. He did this with food and clothing and a listening ear. Life is all about love for Tom as he tries to heal the broken lives around him. It seems to me that if human love, with its deficiencies and flaws, can mend broken hearts and free hearts that have become tough and coarse, then surely God's love, can break through any resistance.

Sadly, we are complex human beings and those of us who follow Jesus like to think of ourselves as being like him, with hearts that are big enough to embrace the leper and the stranger and bring healing and peace. In fact, our attitudes and our actions often show us to be a long way from the paradigm of the Gospel. Ronald Rolheiser, when reflecting on this, writes, 'Too often we have an unconscious mantra that says: I can only be good if someone else is bad. I can only be right if someone else is wrong. My dogma can only be true if someone else's is false. My religion can only be right if someone else's is wrong. My Eucharist can only be valid if someone else's is invalid. And I can only be in heaven if someone else is in hell.' In other words, we become blamers and accusers to try and deflect from our own mess. We try and strengthen the fragile ego which can never face the reality of ourselves and what we can really be like - petty, small-minded individuals who want to put people in hell to satisfy our self-righteousness.

I remember speaking at a day of reflection and at the end of the input, which was about God's love, I had to deal with a long queue of people who wanted to justify their attitude towards others and whose place in hell or purgatory was justified. Most of them did it by calling on dogma, doctrine, canon law and the need for justice in the world. Others used morality, particularly sexual morality, right churchmanship and correct liturgy to justify their position. I am afraid none of it shifted me from my stance that love is enough and in the words of the author Rob Bell, 'Love Wins.'

It is undoubtedly true that, in the bible, it is clear that there are ways of living and being that can separate us from the kingdom of God. Jesus himself talks of issues of justice and the unwillingness to love and forgive as being the means by which we cannot experience the kingdom. Remember the parables of the sheep and goats and the rich man and Lazarus. We must take into account, when reflecting on these parables, a typically rabbinic style of preaching that goes to an extreme to make a point, but it is certainly true that there are stories and passages in the Bible that support exclusion from the kingdom. However, the Bible also makes it clear that God's love for humanity is never ending and encompasses everyone, good and bad alike. The desire of God's heart is that we all, regardless of how we have lived and loved, be somehow brought into the kingdom. We used to have a lecturer at college who would often say, 'you might get a surprise when you realise who you are sitting next to in heaven.'

I was once leading a retreat which was entitled 'an encounter with unconditional love'. At the end of the first session, I was confronted by an angry woman who pushed me against the wall and held me there as she venomously accused me of not believing in God's judgment and justice. Though angry, she was, I think, a good woman. Her life had been hard and when she had become aware of the Gospel, the things Jesus said had led her to give up certain ways of life that had dulled her heart and mind. She screamed at me, 'There has to be justice for the way we have lived our lives. God's retribution has to be fulfilled.' She went on to talk about the amount of evil and suffering in the world and before she burst into tears, she screamed at me, 'someone has to pay. There has to be a hell.' By the way, I had never denied that reality. It is amazing the spin that people can put on things that are said because of their own inner state.

Judgement and retribution, in the way most of us understand those words, are a long way from God's understanding. I would say the notion of God's justice in the scriptures is about love, mercy, forgiveness and restoration. So I tried to say to her that I did not deny the existence of hell, nor of the importance of God's judgment. I suggested that the desire to see other people suffer retribution that was coming across from her had little to do with God. It was more to do with her own need for revenge and punishment on those who were not living as she thought they ought. After a while, when she had calmed down, she began to see that what I had said was true. Much of what she had projected on to God came from a need for vengeance that was within her and had nothing to do with God at all. Too many of us have a need to see those we deem to be wicked punished, and we call that need justice. God loves everything and everybody perfectly and God's justice is perfect; but it is not human justice. As I said earlier, God's justice is tied up with the values of love, mercy and forgiveness and restoration. I have often felt that many people do not like the God of unconditional love, or indeed, do not want unconditional love to be true; but God loves us, pure and simple. It is not in the heart or mind of God to be offended and therefore hold grudges, arbitrarily sending people to hell. There is nothing that any of us can do that can separate us from the love of God. God does not reward or punish us on the basis of whether we have been good or bad. God simply loves us.

I love the stories of the resurrection that we find in John's Gospel. I am convinced that, despite our celebrations of Easter, we lock ourselves into rooms of our own making - bitterness, fear, insecurity, hurt and sin; just like those first disciples were locked in a physical room. Just as Jesus came and stood among them, so he comes and stands within us. As I have written in other books, John is trying to show us a new kind of presence. It is a presence that can come through closed doors, even the doors of our hearts, and is among people like us. It is a presence outside space or time and his greeting to them is Shalom, a word for the Jews that promises fulfilment. In his presence we can find complete fulfilment. Then he shows them his hands and his side. The risen Jesus is still the wounded Jesus. The wounds that he has remind us that we enter into eternity in our wounded state. Jesus brings his wounded humanity before the Father and trusts in the extraordinary nature of love. Most of us, locked in our rooms of insecurity and fear, think we have to be perfect to enter into eternity. Like Jesus, we are invited to come before God and trust God with our weakness and believe that God's gaze of love will bring us to wholeness and peace. That is when we will finally know that we do not have to be perfect to be loved. We just have to trust and believe in the power of love. It is in this love that our sin is forgotten. When we know and believe that we are loved then our sinfulness no longer matters to anyone but us. The forgiveness of sin is about a relationship of love. Our hope in the resurrection is that God will be God. God can only love. That is the nature of God and when we stand before God, we face unconditional love and forgiveness. There are no locked doors through which Christ cannot go.

I have a friend who until recently has been the director of a small hospice. She says that often, those who struggle and fight death the most are deeply religious people. It is usually because they have been fed a wrong image of God, and with it, an image of hell and purgatory. For many of them, their life in Christ has been a matter of earning God's favour in order to achieve heaven. If that is the case, and as death approaches they feel they have fallen short then they can become very afraid of what death means and what they will meet on the other side. Until we recognise the wonder of love in God, then life and death are very frightening. As Richard Rohr says, in that state 'this is not a benevolent universe, but a hostile and dangerous universe where an angry God does not follow his own commandment about love of enemies.'

So what of hell? Pope Saint John Paul II reminded us that heaven and hell are states of consciousness in which we live. All of them are dependent on faith and belief. Hell is that state where love does not penetrate, and the human consciousness does not want it to. God never withholds love that can penetrate any darkness.

The question is, would any human being walk away once seeing and experiencing love, even after death? I think the answer is no, but I guess we all have to make up our own minds. I called this chapter hell, purgatory and love because I wanted to explore these doctrines in terms of a loving God and not as places of punishment where we are sent, as most people sadly seem to see them. As I have already said, I see things in terms of love always being victorious and the desire of God's heart as being the salvation of all not just a few. Richard Rohr says, 'A number of Church Fathers during the first four centuries of Christianity believed in what is called apokatastasis, or 'universal restoration' (Acts 3:21). They believed that the real meaning of Christ's resurrection was that God's love was so perfect and so victorious that it would finally triumph in every single person's life.' I have to say that I find that a beautiful way of expressing the truth of God's love for all creation and a way of expressing the desire of God's heart. Purgatory for people like Julian of Norwich was that state of being where God's extraordinary love could still touch people's lives. I have no idea where we got the picture of clanking chains and souls in agony, epitomised by Jacob Marley in Dickens' Scrooge. Maybe it is because that we are frightened to believe in mercy, unable to cope with a love that is so intense. Perhaps it is part of whatever original sin is, that we believe we have to earn our own salvation and pay for our sins and dare not trust in the power of love. We then create from something beautiful, the mercy and love of God, a place of punishment and atonement that is so dreadful. For me, purgatory has always been that moment of meeting with God and discovering that we have fallen short of the love that flows from the heart of God. The pain of that falling short is almost too much to bear but that pain is instantaneous, and we are cleansed in that encounter and freed. That for me is purgation. Again it is Richard Rohr who writes of purgatory, 'Like many great mysteries, it deteriorated into its exact opposite, a place of punishment—which is all a worldview of scarcity can devise.'

I think the moment of meeting with God will be that moment when we see our lives, and we recognise all the moments of missed opportunity and selfishness and smallness, and the pain of that is our judgement and our moment of purgation. The face of God will reflect, even in the midst of our mess and lack of faithfulness, mercy and love. Will there be judgement on us and on this world? Well, the Scriptures certainly seem to indicate it. But will that judgement be as we tend to understand judgement with our petty, human need to punish and get our pound of flesh? I do not think so.

Many years ago I came across a poem by a blind girl called Kathy Paschal. In it she described what it was like to be blind. She spoke of being locked into a world that others do not understand, a world devoid of colour and vibrancy. Some time ago I watched a TV programme in which a woman, through an accident as a child, had lost her sight. As an adult, she fell and, whatever happened in the fall, her sight was restored. She talked of the wonder she felt at seeing again, but also of the confusion, bewilderment and pain she experienced as she readjusted to a world of sight. Could our encounter with the love of God at the moment of death be seen in such a way? Our 'overwhelming' with the power of love is an experience of wonder, bewilderment and pain that heals and frees and brings with it a purification. Ronald Rolheiser says, 'Might purgatory be understood not as God's absence or some kind of punishment or retribution for sin, but as what happens to us when we are fully embraced, in ecstasy, by God, perfect love and perfect truth?'

My friend Frances is the mother of a large family. She has 11 children and despite occasional differences they all get on well and are good friends. Her youngest daughter, Jody, left home and went to university in another part of the country. When she graduated Jody got a job in a large financial institution. Her mum was aware that she lived life in the fast lane but that was all she was aware of. Jody lived in a lovely flat in central London; she drove a fast car and took expensive holidays. As the years went on contact with her mum and the rest of her family was sporadic. Frances was sad about this, but knew that Jody was

finding her way in life and she, Frances, was just grateful that
life seemed to have dealt her a good hand. Then disaster struck.
Frances was reading the paper and came across an article about
a huge financial scam regarding property and mortgages. In the
middle of the article was Jody's name. She had been found
guilty of fraud and was due to be sentenced the following week.
Frances was there in court when her weeping daughter was
sentenced to seven years in prison. Jody could hardly look at her
mum and told her solicitor that she did not want to see her. After
sentencing all Frances' letters to her daughter went unanswered.
When Jody left the prison, she settled in Ireland, although her
mum had no idea of this. The years went on without any contact.
Despite her other children being around her, Frances mourned
Jody's absence and became a shadow of her former self. Twenty
years passed and Frances was in her mid-seventies. Whenever
I met her, she would weep and talk about Jody's absence
from family life. She just wanted her back, as did the rest of her
family. One evening Frances was cooking tea for two of her
grandchildren. The doorbell went and Frances asked her grand-
daughter to go the door.

The little girl came into the kitchen and told Frances there was
a lady to see her. Frances came to the door wiping her hands on
her pinafore and looked up into the eyes of Jody. Frances threw
her arms around her daughter and sobbed. Eventually she led
the girl into her house and introduced her to the two grandchildren there. Then she phoned each of her children who, one
by one, rushed around to see Jody. There was not an ounce of
recrimination in any of their hearts. Much later on when I met

Jody, she told me that the love she experienced from her family was almost too overwhelming. She talked of their love and her shame. She said the moment her mum put her arms around her, every single moment that she had been in prison flashed through her mind. She spoke of being elated by love but very much aware of her own failings, and the pain of it all was excruciating. Love however was strong enough to heal Jody, to hold Jody and to bring her new life. Jody was restored. That for me is what purgatory is all about.

We can never be more loving than God; it is not possible! As Richard Rohr says, 'If you understand God as Trinity, the fountain and fullness of outflowing love, relationship itself, there is no possibility of any hatred in God. Finally, God, who is Love, wins.' Every single one of us is saved by love and by mercy, that undeserved kindness which flows from the heart of God. Knowing that this is how God deals with us should give us courage as we face the future. So, there is no need to be afraid of meeting God because all we will ever meet is love. Hell and purgatory have no hold over us because of the power of love. We simply have to trust and believe in that love. We do not have to live in fear, but from love. I think that is what Paul means when he asks in the letter to the Corinthians 'death where is your victory, grave where is your sting' To the degree you have experienced intimacy with God, you will not be afraid of death because you know the power of God's overwhelming love.

FOUR

LOVE SETS US FREE

I WAS RECENTLY INVITED TO OUR LOCAL COMMUNITY FELLOWSHIP to hear a woman from America speak. I was told that she had an extraordinary story and indeed she had. Mary is a genuinely nice, ordinary woman, married and divorced with three teenage children to bring up. She had a mortgage and all the usual financial burdens that most people have but she managed to get by. She had worked for one of the big American financial institutions for many years and was a respected colleague and a good worker. One day, Mary went into the bank after her usual busy morning, getting the children ready for school and arranging everything she needed to sort before the day began.

When she got to her desk, her phone was ringing and her line manager asked her to come to his office. Mary was told there was a discrepancy in some figures she had prepared and that the matter would have to be investigated. She was told to leave the office and take all her personal belongings with her. Mary's world was turned upside down that day. As the months went by, it became apparent to her that she was caught up in a fraud of which she was entirely innocent but did not know how to prove that innocence. She was eventually arrested, charged with fraud, and went to court. Despite protesting her innocence, she was sentenced to three years in prison and ordered to pay the bank back the money she had supposedly stolen. She lost her home, her children were placed in care, all of them devastated by what had happened. Mary went to prison where she grew increasingly bitter towards the bank and the justice system that had sent her to prison.

When she left prison, she was placed in a hostel, but the time came for her to leave there. She had nowhere to go and was on the streets for a while and all the time her bitterness and anger grew until they almost consumed her. Her probation officer had got her a job while she was in the hostel but when she lost her place there, she lost her job too. Alone and desperate, she cried out to the God she doubted existed. It was the last thing she would do because she had decided to take her own life the next day. God showed up. She described being filled with a warmth and an awareness of the presence of something more than herself. Bewildered at what had happened, she walked for a while until she found herself outside a church. She went in and found a group of people who welcomed her and listened to her story. One of the people there sensed her genuineness and took her home, and from that point, her life began to change in very practical ways; she found another job and rented a room in a house where her children could visit. She told us that the most extraordinary thing had happened to her when she cried out to God; the warmth of love had melted the corrosive bitterness that had entered her heart. She said that she still faced many issues and was still trying to prove her innocence, 'but' she said, even if she was unable to do that, 'finally, I am free.'

Deep inner freedom is, I believe, the gift of God. That freedom does not depend on the circumstances in which we find ourselves. It is not dependent on how we feel or do not feel. It is gift, pure and simple, and all we have to do is want it and it is ours. I am drawn back to the book of Exodus which I know I have written and spoken about many times. It is the great biblical story of liberation; but it seems to me that just as it is central to the First Testament, so it is central to our understanding of the amazing love of a God who wants to set us free. It is not just the story of a motley group of slaves freed by an ancient Pharoah but a symbolic telling of the desire of God's heart that all God's people be free, that you and I be free. The journey of Exodus reflects the journey that everyone makes when we set out in faith to discover God's love and God's desire that we know deep inner freedom. Just as the ancient people of Israel discovered a radical love that set them free, so can we.

Laurence or Lol Pennington was a man I met in my first pastoral appointment after ordination. He had experienced that radical freedom. He had sparkling eyes and a ready smile always played around his lips. He was married with four children and was one of the stalwarts in the parish where I lived. As I got to know him, I discovered one of the freest men I have ever met. He was completely free from what others thought about him or felt about him. He was comfortable in whatever company he found himself. The poorest of the poor and the richest of the rich were all the same to Lol. He prayed each day and listened for the impulses of the spirit in his life and always followed them. He had encountered the love of God in the Catholic Young Men's Society. That had been built on when he encountered

Charismatic Renewal in the 1970's, and that love had set him free from so much until he was the person I met in Thatto Heath, St Helens. He loved God and God's people. He was to be found helping others whenever he could. He was a Eucharistic minister and a member of the Knights of St Columba, a Catholic organisation that tries to meet people's needs. Through those ministries, Lol prayed with, and worked for others. He was direct and honest and could be uncomfortable to be around because he was so free. The parish priest at the time was a little bit frightened of him because of his experience of God's love, an experience which I think was more than the priest could cope with. When Lol died, the church was full as people came to thank God for the gift of this wonderfully free man and the way in which his life had touched so many people.

It is obvious that in the book of Exodus, Egypt is the place of slavery and the Promised Land the place of freedom. The experience of Israel's journey to freedom is the same radical journey into which we are called as God liberates us. On this journey to freedom, we are invited to discover our own personal Egypt, discover where we are held in slavery and then open ourselves to experience the saving, freeing power of love. Inner freedom only comes when we want love and are willing to trust love more than anything else.

The book of Exodus is far more than a literal story as it explores religious truth which is always eternal. If it is not about religious truth, leading us into the mystery of a God who loves us and frees us, then much of what we read seems a long way removed from our experience. It is hard to believe the things that we read happened as the author says they did, and if we take it all literally, then the temptation is to say that God worked wonders then but not anymore; God freed people then but not now; God loved people then, but it is a different story today!

Of course, the truth is that God's love is not subject to time and space and what these ancient stories are trying to do is help us make connections. They are trying to enable us to see God at work in our lives just as the ancient Israelites saw God at work in their escape from Egypt. The Israelites experienced God's saving love at work in their lives because they reflected on what happened to them and saw the power of love at work. For example, there was a perfectly natural explanation for the way in which the Red Sea parted before the Israelites. It has something to do with the crossing of tides. Some scholars say that the Israelites crossed the Sea of Reeds, which is a swampy area in the northern part of the Red Sea. Because they were on foot they walked through quite easily while the Egyptians on horseback and in carriages sank into the mud. Whatever happened, the Israelites looked at that experience and saw the presence of God in it. They saw the power of love freeing them. As they passed the story from generation to generation, the walls of water got bigger and bigger. We seldom reflect and recognise the presence of God. Yet not to do that means we can miss the truth of God's love amidst ordinary life.

The scholars tell us that whatever the Exodus was, it happened somewhere between 2000 and 1200 BC. It seems that those who escaped were a group of individuals who were enslaved together. What made them a people and gave them an identity was the experience of Exodus and their encounter with the amazing love of a God who wanted to set them free. They were led out of Egypt by the faith of one man, Moses. Basically, Moses is a well-educated man, a Hebrew by birth but brought up as an Egyptian prince, who commits a murder, runs away and then has an experience of God in which he feels called back to Egypt to set God's people free.

His experience of God is symbolised by the story of the burning bush in Exodus chapter 3. It says something powerful about God. God is luminous and alive with a radiance that can never die. God is the fire that will never go out, and so God is eternal. God is amazing love, and that love burns like the bush and can never be extinguished. Maybe, like Moses we have to learn to take off our shoes because we are always on sacred ground.

Rick Warren, the evangelical preacher, once wrote, 'The more you believe and trust God, the more limitless your possibilities become for your family, your career - for your life.' Trusting love and taking risks are right at the core of our faith journey. To risk and trust is what enables love to work in our lives and to become the most important reality there is. We see that risking, trusting, and opening to love in Moses' story, as God does not tell him how to lead the people out of Egypt but simply says, trust me. The more Moses trusts in God's love and in his experience of God the more God works in his life. The same is true for us. If we have encountered love, then we are to trust it and we will experience more love even in hardship and difficulty. The more we are willing to outstare the darkness, as Sheila Cassidy puts it in her book 'Sharing the darkness,' the more we will know the amazing love of God sustaining us and freeing us.

Mrs Roberts worked in our local area as a cleaner. She lived in some council maisonettes not far from us. She had lots of children and her husband did not work. Some people thought he was feckless, but I thought him a nice man, probably because he always had a sweet or two in his pocket for little boys and he was able to carve small wooden animals with a penknife. That meant his wife had to clean to make ends meet. She got up early in the morning to work in city centre offices, and then went back to those same offices in the evening. During the day, she worked in people's houses and had quite a good reputation for being quick and efficient. Her life was far from easy. Her mother was bed ridden and lived with the family. I remember once going with my mum to sit with the old lady who, at the time, needed medication to be given. While Mrs Roberts was out cleaning; Mr Roberts had to put his bet on and could not look after the old lady. Mrs Roberts' mum lay in a big bed in the middle of the front room and, while clean, the house was very bare and the old lady had threadbare coats piled on top of her to keep her warm. The old lady kept shouting out for Queenie. I later discovered that was Mrs Roberts' name. She then messed the bed and mum sent me out into the yard while she dealt with the matter. By the time I got back inside, some of the children and their friends had arrived home from school and it was bedlam as they ran around screaming and shouting, playing cowboys and Indians, which I joined in. The old lady was still crying out for Queenie. There were kids whooping and roaring, others crying because they were hungry and tired and there seemed to be no food around. As soon as Mr Roberts got back from the betting shop, I was unceremoniously grabbed and pulled away from a little girl I was about to scalp. It was time to go and leave the noisy house behind. Queenie Roberts had a hard life. She never moaned or complained about her lot. She was always cheerful, smiley, and willing to help anyone else that she could. Each morning as she left for the first of her office jobs, she went to 7am Mass in St Mary's, Highfield Street and it was that which sustained her. At Mass, every day, she met unconditional love and because of that she could cope with everything that life threw at her.

Moses had to face the hardness of Pharaoh and the securities of the system, but he trusted in love. Even when the ten plagues happened, which from the perspective of faith become events through which God worked, Moses trusted in God's love to set the Israelites free. As I am sure you know over the years the stories were exaggerated, but the fact remains that some slaves in the most powerful empire of the world were set free. God freed the oppressed and all the stories that go with it are illustrations of the miraculous work God did in setting them free. Is that not an indication of the extraordinary love that God has for God's people?

I am quite sure at the time the Israelites were encountering God, they did not recognise what God was doing, but in hindsight they did and so they wrote down the story of God's saving power to encourage us to believe in that same love. One of my greatest friends says that the greatest sight God has given us is hindsight, because it is in looking back through our lives that we see the presence of God at work. It is with hindsight that we recognise what God is doing in our lives and how love is constantly liberating us and setting us free. When we are in the experience, we do not always see. In fact, usually we cannot see God at work at all; we simply have to trust. Faith is not about certitude. It is about feeling the way and believing in the love and the promise of God. I know dogma and doctrine are important. They provide the framework in which we operate but it is far more important to trust in the living God whose love is active in our lives even when we do not feel it or, at times, expect it.

As we see the Israelites move off into the desert, that challenge to trust is of paramount importance. They had no idea where they were going. What does it mean to say they were heading for the Promised Land? 40 years in the Sinai desert on a journey should only have taken them eleven days. They had to learn the lesson of trusting in the love that led them out of Egypt and which would be with them for ever, guiding and leading. It is a reminder to us that we are required to trust in love on this journey of faith. Each one of us will have our times in the desert. We will all have times when we experience being overwhelmed but will we trust in love? As Ronald Rolheiser says, 'trusting in love is the acid test of faith.'

The challenge is always to be a person of faith, to grow in trust day by day, to be formed by, and believe in, the love we have experienced. That is the essential lesson of the desert. When the Lord sends manna from heaven to Israel, he tells Moses to tell the people only to pick up enough food for themselves for the day. What is that saying if not 'Trust in love'? That lesson always goes against the grain because we always want to plan; but the lesson is to let go, give up control and surrender to the Lord so that we can increasingly experience this love freeing and transforming us.

After the Israelites go through the Red Sea the writer of the book says this in chapter 14:31: 'the people put their faith in Yahweh and in his servant Moses.' Trust in God goes hand in hand with trust in other people. We often discover the extraordinary love of God through community. When I was ill with depression, it was those who held my hand in the darkest moments and listened to my incoherent ramblings who revealed the love of God to me. The faith life of any community is built on love and trust. In a Christian community, it is built on the foundations of faithfulness to God and to the others with whom we share this life of faith. The story of the Ten Commandments describes how the Israelites were to be faithful to God and to one another, and I would like to reflect on them because they clearly illustrate the love of God for us.

The Ten Commandments sum up all the law in the book of Exodus. Those who accept the first three commandments say that they will trust God. In a way those who accept the last seven are saying that they are willing to trust one another. The first commandment sums up all ten: 'I am the Lord your God. You shall have no other Gods beside me.'

In the Bible there is only really one sin and that is idolatry which means the making of something into God that is not God. If that is the case, then very few people are guilty of sin in the Biblical understanding. Why? Because you cannot want other Gods once you have met the real God, you cannot be unfaithful to a personal relationship unless you have one and most people, sadly, do not have that sort of relationship with God. How can you be unfaithful to something you have never had?

That does not mean that people do not do things that are wrong or bad. They do, but they are not sinning in the Biblical sense. We are called to fall into grace, to fall into love and to respond with love, to have a personal relationship with God. Once we experience and know God's love for us then we are capable of sin. Personal relationship brings with it a new responsibility. There is a sense in which we have a right to expect more from believers than from non-believers.

One of the lessons of the book of Exodus is that of trusting in love, and there is a sense in which that is captured by the third commandment, which tells us to keep holy the Lord's Day. The people of Israel were to rest on the seventh day of every week. It was a day set apart for us to realise that God is the real power in our lives and only in that power can we trust. In a sense, what God is saying to us is that for one day a week, we are to stop

achieving or doing and trust in God. The third commandment
has got nothing to do with rules of what kind of work we can or
cannot do on a Sunday. That legalistic interpretation covers up
the real message of the third commandment which is simply
this: for one day of the week stop going your own way and trust
in God's love.

If we then take a glance at the last seven commandments, we
discover that they are all about relationships between people.
They are the minimum that must be observed if people are going
to live together. Children are to appreciate their parents; married
people need to avoid adultery; honesty and truthfulness are the
kerbstones of community; people cannot go around killing or
stealing. Trust is the foundation of a community. The Israelites
saw these ethical requests as coming from God and they knew
that as far as they responded to them, they would hear the
deeper word of God's love in their hearts. If we can only learn
to love God and one another and treat one another well, then
we will encounter God in the love we have. Sadly, what we call
the commandments became yet another legalistic hoop to
jump through rather than a means to encounter love and freedom. That is why in Matthew's Gospel Jesus goes beyond the
commandments to a new law written in our hearts that we call
the Beatitudes which free us to live in the power of love. That is
what the commandments were always meant to do.

I love the imagery of the pillar of fire which leads the Israelites
back into the desert and the pillar of cloud which, in the First
Testament, is always a symbol of the presence of God. The pillar

of fire takes us back to Moses' encounter with the burning bush and the imagery that it reflects. It is as if it is reminding us that if we keep our eyes fixed on the love of God then all will be well. Our journey to the Promised Land is never straightforward, but we can discover that land here and now if we stay focused on God's love and search for that love in every encounter and experience we have. When the pillars of fire and cloud stopped, the people of Israel had to stop, and they did not move forward until God led them forward. The lesson of trust and responding to love takes time but it is the way to discover what life and love are about. When we have to stop it is a chance to reflect on where we have been, how we have encountered love and to gather strength for the next stage of the journey. The lesson of God's timing is a long and difficult one to learn, but if we are to experience the Promised Land, it is a lesson to be learnt.

Moses never enters the Promised Land but if you look at what he experienced and encountered in his relationship with God, he did not have to. He had encountered love. He had been set free from his fear. He knew the extraordinary truth of the unconditional, freeing love that is in the heart of God for all humanity. The challenge of the book of Exodus is to open up to love and know that it can set us free. It is the most radically transformative experience that we can possibly have. Try not to get caught up with the legalism, piety, or self-indulgence of much of religion, but let it lead you into the wide, spacious, bountiful arena of love that knows no beginning and no end.

FIVE

THE EVOLUTION OF LOVE

P HILOMENA WAS A WOMAN WHO MY MUM MET IN THE 1960'S at a parish meeting. She worked in a Catholic bookshop in the centre of the city. She was a tall angular woman who had never met anyone who loved or cherished her. She had been brought up very strictly by her aunt, as a matter of duty, because both her parents were dead. School in the 1950's was not much fun and certainly not the place to experience love and affirmation. All of this had made Philomena quite sour and, at times, she could be very caustic in the way she spoke, particularly if she felt threatened in any way. My mum seemed to attract broken people and Philomena found her way into our lives, as did many others down the years. She would often have an evening meal with us but would be gone before my dad got home so he never had to endure the experience which meant he could not blame mum for anything later. Even though we did not have much, Philomena was welcome to share what we had. The times she spent with us were always fraught with tension because of her anger and the manner in which she spoke to us. She was particularly difficult with Paul, my brother. She would criticise him from the time she arrived until the time she left. I think I was probably too small to pick up the sarcasm, but the tension did not escape me.

Many years later I asked mum about Philomena, and she simply

said she was a poor, broken woman who needed our help.
Philomena met Mike at another parish gathering. He was about
the same age as her and seemed to be attracted to her. Philomena
did everything she could to dissuade him. She could not believe
that Mike cared for her at all, let alone loved her, and it took
many years before he broke down her barriers and she began to
believe that it was possible for someone to love her. They got
married when they were in their fifties and, I hope, enjoyed
a good life together. It sometimes takes a while for love to
penetrate.

If we read the Bible from beginning to end, what we have is
a progressive revelation, or maybe it is a progressive realisation on our part, of the loving non-violence of God. This is a
revelation that ends in Jesus who shows a God of radical
non-violence. Even his death on the cross is a teaching on
non-violence. That, I think, blows our minds. We are so violent,
not just in our actions but in our language and in the way in
which we treat one another.

It was Ghandi who said, 'non-violence is not a garment to be put
on and off at will. Its seat is in the heart, and it must be an
inseparable part of our very being. . . . if love or non-violence be
not the law of our being, the whole of my argument falls to
pieces. . . . belief in non-violence is based on the assumption that
human nature in its essence is one and therefore unfailingly
responds to the advances of love. . . . if one does not practice
non-violence in one's personal relations with others and hopes
to use it in bigger affairs, one is vastly mistaken'.

Our mistaken idea of the God of the First Testament who, it appears, orders the extermination of whole peoples, is at best primitive and almost superstitious. This is especially true when it is placed beside the concept of the Father of Jesus who so loved the world that he became flesh, a helpless baby. That baby became a man who was willing to do anything for the sake of love and compassion and died helpless before a baying, angry crowd.

The God who Jesus reveals is free of all violence, and so for those of us who follow Jesus, non-violence has to be one of the cornerstones in the way in which we live. I guess it means that we no longer do violence in God's name. Have we ever really learnt that lesson?

There are lots of examples in the scriptures that show this to be true. The one that always springs to mind comes from John's Gospel in chapter eight, the story of that poor woman who has been caught in adultery. She is brought to Jesus by a crowd of pious Jews who tell him that they have caught her in the act of committing adultery. It is such a trap. They tell Jesus that Moses, who is their primary interpreter of God's will, has ordered that she be put to death for this offence.

Jesus says nothing, but he bends down and begins to write on the ground with his finger. When he is finished, he looks up and says, 'Let the person among you without sin cast the first stone!' Then Jesus bends down and writes for a second time with his finger. One by one, John tells us that they begin to understand and lay down their stones and go away.

Ronald Rolheiser, the Canadian oblate says, 'The key for interpretation of this story is Jesus' gesture of writing on the ground with his finger. Who writes with his finger? Who writes twice? God does, writing with his finger; twice! What God wrote are the ten commandments, and God had to write them twice because Moses 'broke' them the first time. Coming down the mountain, carrying the tablets of the commandments, Moses caught the people in the very act of committing idolatry. Gripped in a fever of religious and moral fervour, Moses broke the tablets of stone on the golden calf and on peoples' heads.'

Moses was violent at this point in the story of Exodus. It is as though he thought he could carry out God's work with a violent reaction. When he climbed the mountain again, there is a moment of revelation when God tells him not to stone the people of God with the commandments! In other words, do not execute violence in God's name!

The people who wanted to stone the woman caught in adultery understood Jesus' action of writing in the sand. He was, in effect, saying that Moses had it wrong. That was so shocking for the Jews who had gathered there.

I want to spend some time in this chapter focusing on the book of Joshua because it is within that book in the First or Old Testament that we have the most problematic images of

God. When we are reading the book of Joshua, and reading particularly the stories of violence and bloodshed, just remember the call to non-violence and the progressive revelation, or realisation, of the loving non-violence of God.

The book takes its name from its central character, Joshua, son of Nun, the faithful helper of Moses. He is the designated leader of the Hebrew people as they take possession of Canaan, the Promised Land. As I said in the last chapter, Moses never entered the Promised Land, probably because he did not need to. He had already encountered the Lord. Thinking of that always reminds me of a book by the Jesuit writer John Powell, called 'Happiness is an Inside Job.' You see, the Promised Land lies within us and the invitation for us is to do battle with those things within that would stop us experiencing that deep shalom which is the hallmark of the Promised Land. It is illustrated in graphic detail by the battles that the ancient people enter into, but it is our battle as much as theirs.

Through Joshua, the leadership of Moses is continued. So, in the book of Joshua there are moments that echo the story of the great Exodus from Egypt; the crossing of the Red Sea in chapters 3 and 4 and in chapter 2 the renewal of the covenant at Shechem a reminder of Sinai. Through the story of Joshua, the author(s) of the book continues the early history of Israel, recounting the fulfilment of the promise of land possession, a promise which stands at the heart of the Deuteronomistic history.

So let us have a look at that Deuteronomistic History. The book of Joshua is part of a much longer historical record which comes from a particular school of religious thought. Most of the scholars today see the book of Deuteronomy as the inspiration for the historical books which follow it, Joshua, Judges, 1-2 Samuel, and 1-2 Kings. It is the theological understanding of that fifth book of Torah or the law, Deuteronomy, which colours the entire history of Israel all the way through to the time of the Babylonian exile. That understanding is simple; if we are faithful to God's ways then we will receive blessings, and if we are not, then it is disaster upon disaster. It is against this understanding that Joshua is to be read.

It took a long time to put together this record of Deuteronomistic history; some of the scholars say over six hundred years. It is made up of various documents and sources that do not always agree with each other, so you get confusing accounts of the same story told in diverse ways and with different emphases. Probably the most central period in this process, was the reign of King Josiah (620-609 B.C.) who inaugurated a reform strongly influenced by the thinking of Deuteronomy.

However this history might have evolved, the final result is very clear. The accounts of the Israelite monarchy, and what went before the monarchy was instituted, provided the Deuteronomists with a framework in which to explain the country's successes and failures from a particular theological point of view.

The fact that the Assyrians destroyed the Northern Kingdom of

Israel in the eighth century B.C. and then Babylon did the same
in the sixth, was not just about military or political inferiority.
As far the Deuteronomistic history was concerned, it was all
down to the failure of the Israelites to live as a sacred,
covenanted people. Had they done so, they would never have
been defeated. Some of the scholars seem to think that the final
editing of the Deuteronomistic History, which included Joshua,
comes from a period shortly after the destruction of Jerusalem
in 587-586 B.C.

It is the religious or theological perspective on Israel's successes
and failures that fills the book of Joshua. As far as the author
was concerned, because the occupation of Canaan was marked
by success in the invaders' military undertakings, this was
because of their faithfulness to God and God's ways. When God
gave Joshua instructions on how to move into the Promised
Land, it seems that God tells him that, once there, he must 'kill'
everything there, all the men, women, children, and even the
animals.

If we take this text literally, it is absolutely abhorrent to us in
the 21st century. It speaks of an image of God that is everything
that God is not. Rolheiser says, 'But this is not a literal text; it is
an archetypal one. It is an image, a metaphor. I suspect that
someone in an Alcoholics Anonymous programme will more
easily get its message: Killing all the inhabitants of Canaan
means precisely giving away all the bottles in your liquor
cabinet - the scotch, the bourbon, the wine, the cognac, the gin,
the beer, the vodka, and everything else that's there. You cannot

take the Promised Land and still keep a few 'Canaanites' on the
side or you will soon lose the Promised Land.'

I think it is fair to say that the image of taking the Promised Land
also allows us to find the way to enter our true self-image. It can
help us know that we are beloved children of God. It can reveal
to us the profound truth that we are totally and unconditionally
loved by God. Rolheiser goes on to explain, 'In great mythical
literature we see that, usually, before the great wedding where
the young prince and the young princess are to be married so as
to live happily ever after, there first has to be an execution: the
wicked older brothers and the wicked step-sisters have to be
killed off. Why? Because they would eventually come and spoil
the wedding. Who are those wicked older brothers and wicked
step-sisters? They are not different people from the young prince
or princess getting married. They are their older incarnations.
They are also inside of us.'

In other words, they are the voices that we begin to hear from a
young age. They are the voices that implicitly tell us we are not
good enough, fast enough, or clever enough. They are the voices
which make us pretend so that we can be acceptable. They come
in many different guises; our mums and dads who by inference
made us feel that we did not quite measure up; or the teacher,
with his or her expectations of what it means to be acceptable.
Bad experiences of the Church which focus on negativity and
sin, shaming us and filling us with guilt that made us fearful
and anxious, can be another voice. That strong, powerful voice,
with its moral authority, has alienated different groups of people

- women, gay people, divorced and remarried - crying out not good enough, not good enough. So we pretend either that we do not care and walk away, or that we fit in. Sometimes it has been in and through the church that we have developed an unhealthy image of God, as we have picked up in the ether that we would not get to heaven unless we jumped through hoops. It is as though our living in heaven had nothing to do with God and everything to do with the number of rosaries or devotions we say. We also hear the voice of society with all its expectations of what it means to be a success, so that unemployed people, street people and people with mental health problems are written off. It is that same voice which condemns the refugee and the asylum seeker for fear they might shake the political and economic status quo. We begin to believe the lie that we have to be a certain shape to fit in and be acceptable. There are so many voices that make us believe from an early age that we are not good enough, and so we learn to pretend and play the games. We begin to believe the illusion we have created for ourselves and even though it is a false illusion, we want to cling on to it and hold it because the fear of rejection is too great to bear.

All of those voices are within us. So the journey we are invited to take is to recognise that we are wonderful creations of God. Not because we are perfect, but because God has created us and loves us as we are. God does not condemn us for who we are. Sadly, the people of Israel were not able to recognise at this stage that God's love was infinite and boundless, and so they saw God's love being offered to them in terms of an agreement. God's love was always unconditional; they were just unable to see that and so God took them as they were. They had a tit- for-tat mentality - God will bless us if we obey the commandments and, if we do not, then God will punish us. It was all about earning God's love and storing up enough merits to make sure that they outweighed their faults. Catholics have been especially prone to this sort of thinking, but really all it does is make the focus what we do rather than what God does. We love to take refuge in this sort of understanding because we can control it. We are not good at unconditional. We deal in terms of black, white, good, and bad.

God is always bigger and more than we care to imagine. God does not deal in black and white and in and out. God can be trusted with mess. We do not have to earn the love of God - it is freely given and does not depend on us. There are so many people stuck in this stage of development, where faith is identified with obeying the commandments and performing the correct rituals in order for God to be pleased with us.

Many years ago I met a man called Alex. He had been married three times and had 14 children, six with his first wife and four each with his subsequent wives. He was a good faithful man but a trifle eccentric. He lived near Scarborough with his third wife, and within each of his families there were mental health issues. Alex's life was spent trying to help his children, along with his third wife who several people described as a saint. Central to Alex's faith was a deep love for the Eucharist. Alex went to mass every day, and would serve; if he did not serve would read the scriptures for the day. So he was a good, faithful man trying to

live his life in the best way he could. I met him at a retreat, and
on the last day he came to me full of apologies that he had to
leave early before the final celebration of the Eucharist. Then
he said something which, to me, was very strange. He said, 'I
suppose it doesn't really matter; after all I have plenty in stock.'
He went on his way but the more I reflected on what he said I
realised that he had fallen into the trap of believing that he had
to earn God's love by going to mass every day. He saw faith as
a balance sheet with numbers of masses, devotions, rosaries on
one side and what he saw as his sins on the other. One had to
outweigh the other in order for God to love him. How sad that
he thought that way, and how much freer he would have been
had he only known that it was all about God's love and nothing
he could do would earn that love in any way.

The book of Joshua brings to fulfilment the promise initially
made to Abraham in the book of Genesis. That promise was
twofold: he would have many descendants and the making of a
great nation would take place. It is with the last part of
that promise that the book of Joshua deals primarily, that is the
occupation of Canaan, the Promised Land. Canaan was a land
where many cults abounded, especially the worship of fertility
gods. It is clear throughout that the Hebrews saw any form of
religious compromise as absolutely excluded from their way
of life. That was the only way in which they could earn God's
love. To highlight the exclusivity of God the book ends with a
ceremony of covenant renewal.

There are two main sections in the book of Joshua. The first deals with the occupation of the land of Canaan in chapters 1-12. The account of the occupation does not extend to the entire territory which later made up the country but is more limited and centred around the land of the tribe of Benjamin. The stories of the way in which the land was taken are considered very ancient, probably dating from the twelfth century B.C., whereas the text dealing with land distribution dates from the time of the established monarchy. The second section deals with the distribution of the land to the twelve tribes in chapters 13-21. The final chapters deal with a dispute regarding a Trans-Jordanian altar in chapter 22, the renewal of the covenant, and the death of Joshua.

Is it historically true or not? I guess the answer is we do not really know. The book forms part of the 'historical' literature in the bible, primarily because it is a broad record of the country's origins and early development. This does not mean it actually happened as it was written. The primary purpose of the book is a theology; the authors wanted us to know that the land was a gift from God to Israel and, regardless of the actual circumstances that made this a reality, the basic belief is never compromised. To make the points they want to make, the authors take stories and narratives and put them together in an idealised account of the story of the taking of the land of Canaan. This was to show that God is never outdone in generosity and always keeps God's promises because of love.

Many years ago, just after I was ordained, the old car I was driving began to breathe its last. It was a Toyota Corolla with many thousand of miles on the clock and I had no idea how I was going to replace it. I needed the car to get between the two schools where I was chaplain, and on to the town youth service that we ran at night. One night it began to judder badly, and I just got back to the house I was living in when the engine stopped completely. As I much as I tried, I could not get the engine to turn over. The next day I asked a mechanic, a friend of mine who had kept the car on the road for a long time, to have a look at it and he told me what I already knew in my heart, that the repairs needed would cost more than the car was worth. I had no idea what to do. For about a week, I managed to scrounge lifts and get the bus. I borrowed a car a couple of times and I prayed. I got home one night with my arms full of bags and folders and dropped them on the floor as I went into the hall, and I began to cry out of frustration. It was all too much for me. When I had finished crying, I saw an envelope on the hall table with my name on it. When I opened it, there was a hand-written note which said 'God thought you might need this.' Bundled up with the note were fifty £50 notes. I had the money for a car. I never found out who did this, but I do believe it was given as a reminder to me that God is loving, and that God will never be outdone in generosity.

While Joshua was obviously an important figure at the time of the conquest, I do not think that we can really hold that he was responsible for all the remarkable strides taken in this book. He is presented as the idealised hero of the conquest and the one who presided over the subsequent distribution of the land. But the fact is that much of the activity presented in the first twelve chapters is localised, and only really relates to the tribe of Benjamin and the land around the sanctuary at Gilgal. The land of Canaan was brought under control only after a century of Israel slowly but surely expanding, and the account of the way in which the land was divided up really comes from a later date when the monarchy had been instituted.

Despite this, Joshua stands as a larger-than-life figure. I think it would be fair to say that he has been drawn to some events recorded in this book more in spirit than in fact. It is under the mantle of his leadership, rather than the reality of his presence that the events of the occupation of the land find their setting. What we find in this book is that God takes the people of Israel where they are and slowly leads them to an increasing awareness of unconditional love.

SIX

GOD IS YOUR LOVER

N ELL DEVIN WAS A WOMAN I KNEW WHEN I WAS GROWING
up. When I was a child, she would look after me,
when mum was working, in her pensioner's flat
which was scrupulously clean, and it was there that she would
mend clothes while I played around. The handover always took
place at morning mass. I would be handed over to Nell while
mum went off to work. We would then walk to Nell's flat,
stopping off at the van to buy a bar of chocolate. Nell was a
lovely person, always smiling and very kind, but that smile hid
a lifetime of pain, which I only discovered in my late teens. Nell
had been abandoned as a baby and was placed in an orphanage
where, whilst the sisters were not cruel, neither were they loving
and compassionate. Physical punishment was often meted out,
but such was Nell's gentle, kind personality, that she never
blamed the sisters at all. 'That is just how it was in those days'
she used to say. When she was fourteen, Nell left the orphanage
and was put into service in one of the big houses in Princes Park.
This was an area in Liverpool where wealthy people lived in the
19th and early 20th century. Nell was a scullery maid and, it
seemed, was the butt of everyone's aggression although Nell
being Nell you had to read between the lines to find that out.
The one good thing about that experience was that it was
there Nell met her husband and they eventually married and
left service. They had two boys and were very happy until the
second world war. Both boys were called up and both were

killed. Nell, as was her way, wiped her tears and got on with life. Mr Devin, as Nell always called him, died, she said, from a broken heart. So when we knew Nell, she was to all intents and purposes alone in the world. However, Nell had faith. She was aware of the presence of God within her and the invitation she was given to trust in his presence; and that is what Nell did. Each day, when she awoke, in her traditional way, she would say a morning offering, surrendering her day and her life to God, and then she would trust that the Spirit within would be her strength

When I think of Nell, I am often led to John's gospel and the place where Jesus tells his disciples that the advocate will come to be with them. In Greek, the word we translate as advocate is Paraclete. A Paraclete is one who stood by the little person who was unable to speak for themselves, the one who was powerless and voiceless, and fought their case in a court of law. The disciples were going to be those little ones and the Spirit of Jesus would be the Paraclete, to be with them and to help them as they face the world. Nell was so aware of that presence that she was never afraid. She knew that she was never alone because God is with us. Whenever we have to face difficult times, whenever we feel abandoned or afraid, believe the truth that his Spirit is within us. Nell knew all of that to be true, and in her simple way she lived that out. In her own way she knew intimacy with God. I suppose she taught me that we do not have to look outside ourselves for strength. The Spirit is present within us and if, in our times of crisis, we can only spend a moment drawing on the Spirit's strength, I think we would be amazed at how real that Spirit is. I think she taught me that surrendering to God's presence within is the only way to find true peace. I was recently struck by the words of Ladislaus Boros, a Hungarian Jesuit who writes widely on Spirituality. He once said this; 'There is an inescapable logic in the Christian message: we experience joy quite simply in surrender, in the giving up of our lives.' Nell was a joy-filled woman because of her surrender to God.

I was thinking recently that much of what the scriptures are pointing us to, and which we find so difficult to handle, is the call to surrender to God. I love the story of Jesus' conversation with Nicodemus, a leading pharisee who came by night to see him. Nicodemus was challenged to realise that he had to become part of a new order which involves a letting go of the need to control and the need to be right. It meant he had to be willing to open himself to the power of God's unconditional love if he was to be part of what God was doing in the world. He also had to be willing to let go of manipulation and power that had been the focus for him and the other Pharisees. Letting go and abandonment are the only ways to know the truth of love. 'So, Nicodemus,' says Jesus 'are you prepared to surrender to the power of love.'

Surrender is a massive question for us all to reflect on. Will we surrender to God's Spirit and allow that Spirit to change us or are we happy as we are, too comfortable to move or to have our comfort zones punctured? Are we prepared to be Spirit-filled people who are unpredictable for the sake of love, regardless of social conventions and what other people might think? Nicodemus, caught up with the life he lives and the beliefs he has, is invited to surrender to the power of love. John follows that conversation with an inclusion in Chapter 3:16. An inclusion is a verse that sums up the whole of the Gospel. 'For God so loved the world....' John wants us to know the reality of God's love for us even if we cannot grasp it, and to show how faith in Jesus will lead us into it more deeply. That is what will free us and enable us to live in the Spirit. That is his perception of reality, the only reality there is. You and I know that the core message of the Gospel is that the gift of God is unconditional, and that the absence or presence of any sort of moral standards in our lives is irrelevant to whether God loves us or not. In other words, we do not have to do anything to be loved. God simply loves us, and so we can trust and we can surrender if we choose to. I often think the real transformation that is to take place within us is in the realm of our image of God. Our false images of God that make us see God as anything but bountiful abundance, are the corrosive, destructive images that cause the overpowering sin of our lives, the making of God into our image and likeness. Then we do not have to surrender or open up. The truth is that God wants nothing from you in return for loving you. Everything is gift. John says not to enter into that love is to be condemned. If we remain fixed behind our walls of certitude and power and our need for security, we will remain locked in fear and darkness; it is to live in self-hatred, and self-pity, selfishness, arrogance and pride rather than in the freedom of grace. God does not judge in John's Gospel. We judge ourselves by our failure to respond to Jesus. John tells us that the coming of the light shows up everything for what it is, and some people prefer darkness and run away from the light. Not to live life to the full or to know and share love is to condemn ourselves to something that is less than life. The responsibility for life and love is ours, so, as this conversation between Nicodemus and Jesus about belief and the Spirit comes to an end, the challenge we are given is to focus on Jesus, to believe in him and in the power of love, to surrender to that love. That is eternal life, and it begins now.

So, in order to begin the process of reflection on the scriptural invitation, we have to be willing to let go and to fall into grace. We so want to be in control and manipulate and engineer our lives into what we think they should be. The reality of life is that we are not in control. So all we can do is to let go of those control needs and fall into grace, fall into God. That is the only way to discover the scriptural truth that we are loved with a radical, extraordinary love. Otherwise we will spend our time trying to create a God in our image and likeness that we can handle and cope with.

That falling into grace is like the chasm of your own soul and the chasm of the nature of God opening up, and you are falling into both of them simultaneously. It is then that you are in a new realm of mystery and grace, where everything good happens. In other words, our falling into grace is a process where we move beyond the petty limitations that we put on God and the crazy way we try to earn approval, and let ourselves be loved. As I have often said, moving beyond the boundaries we put on

God is the scandal of grace. That scandal is love poured out and the extraordinary free gift of life in its fullness; overflowing, bountiful, generous, abundant life. It is the very essence of God given to us so that we can live knowing who God is and who we are, and yet not knowing at the same time. It is captured in the gospel images of abundant life which are things like water changed into wine, the mustard seed that grows into a tree, the oil that keeps the lamp burning, the landowner who pays all his workers the same regardless of how long they have worked. Life in its fullness.

So the scriptures want to take us to that place of surrender, but only an awareness of love will do that. Having reflected a little on the story of Joshua in the last chapter I would like to share some thoughts about the Song of Songs and the image of love that the author shares with us. This book is all about surrender and falling into love.

The Song of Songs is very short, only 8 chapters long, but it is full of imagery and cultural understanding that is really very wonderful to explore. Some of its imagery and language are not easy, but I hope we will manage to reflect a little. What can we say about the Song of Songs? It is a raunchy, sexual love-song of evocative beauty with outrageous imagery and huge extravagances. Scholars tell us that it was meant to be sung as a celebration of love, beauty and intimacy. The song was extremely popular within the social and religious life of ancient Israel. In the social world, it was most probably sung as enter-tainment at local celebrations of the various harvest festivals, accompanied by dancing at a village wedding, sung as court entertainment at the royal palace in Jerusalem, or at happy family reunions or gatherings. Religiously, it was probably sung at weddings and celebrations of marriage of various sorts.

In listening to the song, we find that it is speaking not only to us, but about us; and I found myself drawn into the movement of the verses and the atmosphere that it creates. One of the authors that I read said that, 'our imaginations are stimulated, and we begin to identify with the lovers on their journey of love, of self-discovery and of fulfilment.'

So what do we know about the song? The two lovers are creations and are not modelled on real people. We do not know much about them other than their emotional reality. Are they suited to each other? We do not really know because they are not real people acting out a real-life drama in a particular situation. We know nothing about their personalities. What we do know is how they respond to each other, in as much as their responses and feelings are those characteristic of all men and women in love. That means, of course, we can identify with them. They are every man and every woman, like the character in 'A Man For All Seasons.' I suppose that gives them a reality as we read of the passion and cravings that flow through their veins.

I think it would be fair to say that the song is not meant to tell a story. It is not Eastenders or Coronation Street with all the human drama they express. It is a series of poems put together to portray human sexuality and love, and the ultimate victory of that love over any other reality. It reminds us that love is ultimately all that we have and all that matters. In the reflection on these two country lovers, we are pulled into the power of such love. We are reminded that love is the source of life.

The main themes of this wonderful piece of writing are romantic love, courtship, beauty, passion and mutual commitment. It is a gutsy, physical book that takes our imaginations into places that some of us would rather not go because our upbringings have so repressed us. These two country lovers experience everything that those embarking on a deep human and physical relationship experience; the pain of separation, the agonising fear of loss, the little disagreements which become bigger and bigger, the tensions of insecurity and the lovers' quarrels, all of which are part of the stuff of relationships.

Some scholars say that the relationship between the two lovers express something of the image of the relationship between God and humanity. Ultimately, their relationship speaks of a God who is a lover, not angry, petty or judgemental, but one who woos the beloved. Our theological understanding of God as a trinity of persons supports this. It is all about mutuality and abiding love. The early north African church father, Augustine, used the illustration of two lovers to give us an insight into God and the mutual love which binds the three persons of the Trinity together. God totally gives Godself away for the sake of the Son and the Spirit and then receives that same totality of giving back from each of them. This nonstop waterwheel of love which involves total giving and total acceptance, means that God is love. Glen Scrivener teaches at Union School of Theology in the United States, and he supports this image of God when he writes, 'Any talk of intimacy with God must begin with the intimacy that God is. As a community of Persons united in love, the Triune God enjoys eternal communion. Before the foundation of the world the Father delighted in the Son in the bond of the Spirit.' After calling us to a life of intimacy and communion in the image and likeness of God, Scrivener goes on to say, 'Virtually every verse regarding the pre-creation life of God describes the Father focussing his affections and purposes on the Son. Likewise, the Son, in the power of the Spirit, commits himself utterly to the Father. This is the intimacy that both pre-dated and produced the universe. We have come from divine intimacy and are intended for divine intimacy. The Father has created through and for his Son and he has created in order that there might be billions more 'sons', filled with the same Spirit, sharing in this eternal love.'

The Spiritual journey is the same for all of us as we try to discover the mystery of intimacy with God. It takes most of our life to discover that we are accepted and loved and to learn how to accept everyone else. Most of us cannot do this easily because inside ourselves there is so much poor self-esteem and even hatred of ourselves. We so despise ourselves at times that without an out-pouring of the Spirit in our lives, we cannot believe that God is love nor can we believe that we are caught up in a radical union with God. The good news is that the question of union with God has already been resolved once and for all in

Christ. We cannot create union with God from our side so God has already done it in the gift of Christ and the Holy Spirit who dwells within us. We just have to discover that intimacy for ourselves.

The Song of Songs tries to express this union with God in its sexual language and imagery. It tries to communicate intimacy. Just like the two young lovers in the song, God loves, courts, and woos us, desperate for us to know the truth of love. It says something to us about the nature of God and the desire of God. All love is a reflection of the love that is in the heart of God, the love that is an overflowing creative life force. This God is in love with us. God is our lover with the single-minded delight that a lover has for the loved one. I love this passage from the late Cardinal Basil Hume which I have often quoted,

> Always think of God as your lover. Therefore God wants to be with you, just as a lover always wants to be with the beloved. God wants your attention, as every lover wants the attention of the beloved. God wants to listen to you, as every lover wants to hear the voice of the beloved. If you turn to me and ask - 'Are you in love with God?' - I would pause, hesitate and say, I am not certain. But of one thing I am certain: that God is in love with me.

It seems to me that we can ask as many questions as we like about what that might mean, but ultimately we have to choose whether or not we will open ourselves to love, whatever it is about and wherever it might lead us.

I know I spend a lot of time talking and writing about love. It is not because I cannot think of anything else to say. It is because I know that the core of the gospel message is love and anything else is just 'gilding the lily.' Sadly I think most of us spend a lot of time and energy going down fruitless paths while searching for God. Not that going down those paths is wasted energy, because God is somehow using all that we experience to help us see and draw us closer into the mystery that is divine love. Even our sin and our mess can enable us to see more clearly. Nothing is wasted if we reflect on it and allow it to teach us.

As I have travelled around, it is very clear to me that it is only the deep, radical experience of grace that sets human beings free psychologically, spiritually, and emotionally. It is when we know that we are the objects of God's desire, that we are unconditionally loved, that we really begin to experience life. It is then that we have the courage to surrender and begin to understand the desire of God, the heart of God, that we know life now and forever. Without that knowledge, I think most people live in prisons of our own making. We become narrow, judgemental people who blame and scapegoat. We stay locked into our hurts, our pain, our anger and our frustration, and we can become sour, petty individuals who project on to others what we hate about ourselves. I find it a real sadness that most human beings live within that reality, even those of us who say we have faith. We are caught up in petty moralising, not able to get a glimpse of God's desire for us - that we know love. We have managed to reduce the gift of God into a prize to be earned - the better we are the more we will get. Instead of living in that free place of love poured out and received, which means to live in a world of abundance and open horizons, we live in small petty worlds where our own ego is the only reality that motivates us. We spend most of our time striving to get more of God; and God has already poured out everything for us. God has given Godself away because we are the desire of God's heart. Read the Song of Songs, it will take your breath away.

Grace is really very crushing to the ego, because it is free; and we want to earn it and measure it and we cannot do that; it is gift; it is the work of the Spirit; the love of God is poured out. We are forgiven, freed, saved, whatever language we care to put on it. The heart of God is love flowing out and there is nothing we can do to earn it. If only we knew that to be true.

So through the experience of these two lovers, we get an insight into God's longing for us. Chapter 4:1-7 are interesting because in them, we have the first occurrence in the song of what is called in Arabic, a wasf. This is a poem of praise in which one of the lovers describes metaphorically, the other's bodily parts in a catalogue moving from head to toe or vice-versa. This type of poem is one of the characteristics of Arabic love poetry, but it only occurs in the Old or First Testament in the song of songs. The lovers find each other beautiful and attractive, and the metaphors used to describe that beauty are just something we have to get used to. It has been suggested that some of the descriptions fit more aptly the description of an artist's picture of the beloved, or a statue, or a model. He says that she is altogether lovely and every part of her is perfect. Her eyes are like gentle doves, her hair flows like goats down a hillside. To us this metaphor is very strange - goats are smelly and dirty and their coats are tangled; but here, the point of comparison is the flowing and rippling movements of the flock down the grassy slopes. From a distance the jostling flock bobs and weaves in glistening undulation, just as her flowing locks do as she walks and turns. He says that her teeth are like newly washed sheep and her lips like scarlet ribbon. Nice! It just illustrates how little we know about the culture in which these ancient books are written. He looks forward to spending the night exploring her fragrant mountains. The song is loaded with eroticism.

I remember hearing a phrase that John Shea the American storyteller used when addressing a congregation. He said 'you are full of grace, and you do not know it.' We do not know the beauty that lies inside us, and we do not see ourselves in the way God sees us. Our veils are not just physical; they are emotional, psychological, intellectual and spiritual. We all wear masks to protect our insecurities. We are afraid of what we think is weakness, and we despise our vulnerability instead of seeing it as our greatest gift. Just as the girl progressively unveils herself to the boy, maybe we are being challenged to let go of our masks so that we can deepen our relationships with God, with others and with creation. When we move into chapter 4:8 through to 5:1; the lover calls his bride to come from the remoteness and dangers of mountain ranges to the intimacy and safety of his love. It is about intimacy, about surrender, about allowing God to be the sort of lover God wants to be. I think the truth that we all know is that it is only God who satisfies and maybe that is one of the lessons to be learnt from this book, that as well as being a beautiful reflection on human love and sexuality, it is also a metaphor for our relationship with God who alone can satisfy our need. Robert Michel, an oblate priest, says this, 'you must try to pray so that, in your prayer, you open yourself in such a way that sometime - perhaps not today, but sometime - you are able to hear God say to you: `I love you!' These words, addressed to you by God, are the most important words you will ever hear because before you hear them, nothing is ever completely right with you, but, after you hear them, something will be right in your life at a very deep level.'

SEVEN

THE PROPHETS OF LOVE

I N THE MIDDLE OF THE MAY BLITZ IN 1941, MANY CHILDREN FROM
Liverpool were evacuated to the much safer Welsh
countryside. One of them was a child called Agnes who was
just twelve. She was originally from Yorkshire and had settled
in Liverpool with her aunt and uncle. She lived with them
because her parents had been tragically killed in a farming
accident. After that, Agnes never felt that she belonged
anywhere. Her upbringing was tough because her aunt and
uncle were not the warmest or the kindest of people and had
only taken on young Agnes because it was their duty. She
experienced a lot of beatings and was frequently hungry. When
the evacuation took place, her guardians were only too pleased
to get rid of Agnes. Agnes often used to talk about Wales as her
salvation because it was there that she met Mrs Jones. Gwyneth
Jones was in her fifties, a widow who radiated kindness and
love, and the young Agnes was welcomed into her home. When
she was bullied in school because of her strange accent, Mrs
Jones fought her corner with a teacher who had no truck with
these incomers from Liverpool. When she was accused of
shoplifting, it was Mrs Jones who stood against the small village
community and was publicly isolated. She stood beside Agnes
in the Magistrates' Court and paid her fine. Love was the only
thing that mattered to Mrs Jones and that love was prophetic in
the way it transformed Agnes. At the end of the war, Agnes's
uncle and aunt could not be found; maybe they were victims

of the blitz. So Agnes stayed in the small Welsh village with 'aunty Gwyneth' until she returned to Liverpool to train at the Royal Infirmary as a nurse. We met Agnes in the 1960s in our parish. At that point she was married but never stopped talking about Wales and aunty Gwyneth.

As a small child, I was taken to see this redoubtable lady and have never forgotten her. She had a huge personality and exuded quiet strength She baked scones with homemade jam and cream and made tea in a huge earthenware teapot. As she bustled around, homespun wisdom fell from her lips, and I will never forget her saying to me, 'Christopher, boy, remember the only thing that matters in life is love, whatever the cost.'

I would like to begin this chapter by reflecting on what it means to be a prophet because it seems to me that we have made it all about predictions rather than about speaking God's radical love into a situation, which I think is probably more what prophecy is about. It is about seeing clearly into the present and speaking what is heard into the world.

Religious Prophets are seldom establishment people. They constantly call traditions into question, which is very necessary if the traditions are not to become ends in themselves and eventually idols. It is sad that so many of our traditions, particularly in the Catholic Church, become ends in themselves. There is only one absolute and that is the Kingdom of Love.

It seems as though the Old or First Testament prophets receive the word of God in two places; firstly at the moment of their call, and then secondly, because of that experience of God, they continue to search for God's word throughout their lives as they read the signs of the times in life, in great political events and in day-to-day living.

From the time of their calling, everything speaks to them of the love of God; the branch of an almond tree in flower, or a boiling pot (Jeremiah 1: 11ff), married life (Hosea1-3; Ezekiel 24:15ff) or enemy invasion. The challenge of the prophets is to allow everything around to speak of God. I guess that is the first challenge they give us. We are invited to look around and see the presence of God in everything. If we do, we cannot fail to believe that God is love. Sadly, we do not follow this practice, and yet the truth of revelation is that God is in all things. Find God in the gift of this world; find God in other people; find God in yourself.

Prophets look into the past and see what God has done in history. They recognise the pattern of God's love, the call to trust and the surprising life given to those who learn how to trust. The pattern they recognise as they look back is always the pattern of salvation; God loving, God calling and God giving new life. As they reflect on the past, the Prophets can also see that when the people were unable to believe in God's love or respond to God's call, they walked into death instead of life and they experienced injustice, oppression and destruction. The prophet also looks at the present to see which pattern can be identified in the world around them. Is it the pattern that leads to life, or is it the pattern that leads to death? If it's the latter, then the prophet will remind people of the truth of love, sometimes in uncompromising language and images, but always pointing to love.

The Prophets were generally optimists because they believed in the power of God's love, and saw it breaking through over and over again bringing salvation and new life, and they believed in it with a passion. They carried a confidence in their hearts that ultimately God would be triumphant. They knew that God was God alone and they were willing to spend their lives in proclaiming his truth.

I learnt that lesson of steadfast faithfulness from a little old man who used to come to our dementia choir with his wife who had Alzheimer's. Tommy was always smiling, always full of good cheer, smartly dressed, and his conversation was always punctuated with phrases like 'God is good' and 'thanks be to God'. Even when his beloved Betty died, he continued to come to the choir with the same cheerful optimism and a belief in God that was unshakeable.

So why are the Prophets so important to us and why should we try to be prophetic? We have narrowed the word sacred to a very small religious word; but what the Scriptures are saying to us is that all things are sacred because God is intimately involved in the world. The Prophets in the Old Testament tried to point the people towards a God who was present in everything. I think that one of our roles as Church in the world is not to point people towards heaven but to help people recognise the incarnate God, the God who is fearless, radical love if we only opened our eyes to look.

One of the main elements in prophetic writing is emotion. It seems to me that what the prophet is doing is revealing the emotion of God, feeling the anger of God, the pain of God, the deep never-ending love of God. Sometimes the Prophet is communicating the ache of God, and you and I know that the ache of our heart is not always rational, but it is very real. I guess that is where the prophet starts because it is only at that non-rational level that change happens and that we can begin to let go of our images of God that would make God anything other than love.

Rational thinking has formed the Western world. It has formed you and me and because of that we find it very difficult to change our image of God. We rationalise it out of existence. Why should we believe in a God of radical love? What evidence is there for such a God? Why should we trust God with our pain? Why should we allow God's love into our hearts? Why should we trust God when God will probably let us down? Why should we be open? It is not rational to be like that but what does each of the synoptic Gospels say to us? Repent! Change the way you think about God. It is almost as though we have to let our rational minds go.

Spirituality operates on the level of the non-rational and for me one of the big problems with religion is that we do not believe in the reality of the spiritual world. We are materialists. We believe in what we can touch, what we can see, and in what works right now. It is crazy because 90% of our lives are motivated by the unconscious. We do not know why we do what we do, why we feel what we feel. The only people who really know are those who have hit rock bottom.

Sadly, we have created a community of people who are afraid to love deeply, afraid of passion, afraid of vulnerability, afraid of the non-rational, and so we cannot hear the voice of God and respond to it at the level the Gospels invite us to respond. The plan of the prophet is to create an alternative consciousness against the culture of the day so that people can be free and know that they are sons and daughters of a radically loving God. So let us take a look at some of the Prophets and the invitation they give us to fall into love. Hosea was preaching in the midst of a lack of faithfulness. He emerged in the final years of the Kingdom of Israel, toward the end of Jeroboam II's reign. Involved in a terrible marriage to Gomer who deserted him for other men, just as Israel has deserted God for the Canaanite God Baal, Hosea, out of his own pain, finds words to express the unfaithfulness of Israel. He tells Israel a parable of her own betrayal of God through his own story. If we can keep that in mind, we will understand Hosea. The first three chapters of the book deliver the message that Hosea has, and the next eleven chapters are fragments of oracles condemning Israel's sin. The book finishes with the beautiful song of Hosea that we know as, 'Come back to me with all your heart.' Hosea understands the pain of a loving God whose love is often ignored.

Jeremiah lived from about 650BC until about 570BC and is one of the great tragic figures of the Bible. His call to be a Prophet came around the year 635 B.C. and he was active during the reigns of the last kings of Judah, Josiah (640 609), Jehoiakim (609-598), Jehoiachim (598-597), Zedekiah (597-587) and continued for some time after the fall of Jerusalem in 587 BC. We know all this because of the paragraph that opens the book of Jeremiah.

He preaches to the Kingdom of Judah, a place that was secure, complacent and arrogant. His message of warning and of the suffering that would most surely come was an unwelcome one. Eventually, Jeremiah comes to realise that it is God's love, compassion and mercy that will never be overcome. It is not about our faithfulness.

The book begins with his call. It is interesting that God never tells him what to say; he simply gives him a call and a promise, which is typical of all the prophetic calls. God calls the Prophet and then promises that Godself will be with him. So Jeremiah sets out with nothing for his journey, and he struggles to find out what he has to do. All he knows is that he got a call and a promise, and that is probably true for most people on a journey in faith. We get a call, somehow, and we get a promise and we live by the promise and we live by the call. Out of that, God creates his victories.

Jeremiah uses an awful lot of images to try and help us confront suffering and to feel the ache of the heart of God for the world. It is almost as though Jeremiah sees that as the vocation of the people of God, to feel the heart of God. Unfortunately many of us think it is about singing nice songs and feeling good about religious things.

Jeremiah uses the Hosea images of the father/son relationship and the husband/wife relationship to call the people back. God is looking for intimacy and faithfulness and trust, and somehow Israel has not been able to sense that. Jeremiah hears God say come back and be healed, return to love, fall into love and find life that can never be vanquished.

Ezekiel was a priest and a Prophet and many of the scholars say that he was the architect of a new Jerusalem, at least in spirit. It is thought that he probably went into exile with the first group of Israelites driven out of Jerusalem in 597 BC. Ezekiel began having visions about five years after arriving in Babylon. His visions were composed of wild images, disturbing warnings, and shocking pronouncements. He has vivid descriptions of idolatry and sexual indiscretions. There are dire threats and powerful depictions of the glory and the name of God. All of it is so that Ezekiel can do what Prophets do and challenge the false theology that makes God into something that human beings can control and handle, and to speak God's word even when it is uncomfortable and shows up stark reality. He sees love as radical and absolute and goes to extremes to shatter people's understanding.

To prepare Ezekiel for ministry three dramatic experiences happen to him. The first is that he beholds the glory of the Lord in chapter 1. In captivity the people of Israel began to wonder and question. Were they not really God's chosen people? Had God really defeated their enemies and given them the Promised Land? Was Jerusalem not the holy city, and the temple God's dwelling place?

There is nothing new under the sun. When we find ourselves in difficult places and life suddenly becomes hard and circumstances are not what we want them to be, we ask the same sort of questions. The first thing Ezekiel needed to understand was that God is love and those who trust will ultimately find life, even in the darkness. God's promise is that one day the city of Jerusalem and the temple will again experience the presence of the Lord or the glory of the Lord.

Ezekiel's second experience comes in chapters 3 and 4 when he accepts the burden of the Lord. One of the truths of the Prophet's life is that somehow they feel the emotion of God, the pain of God and Ezekiel takes that on. It is a huge responsibility. Can you imagine feeling the pain of the world with the intensity of God? So Ezekiel receives his official commission as a Prophet of the Lord God, and the Lord tells him that it is a difficult task that he is taking on.

The third experience is the declaring of the word of the lord in chapters 3 and 4. It is obvious when looking at the history of the people of Israel, that what the people needed more than anything else was to hear the word of God rather than the word of false Prophets. So Ezekiel comes to declare God's word. He comes as a messenger. The people of Israel were the ones to whom the message was proclaimed, and the Word of God was the message to be delivered: God will never give up on Israel; God will never give up on us, always pursuing us, always looking for us to fill us with love. What wonderful news.

Yet, we are so fickle. We say we believe in God; we say we love God and God is the centre of our lives; and yet the first thing most of us do when there is a crisis in our lives is to look towards other things to be our strength and to help us get through. It is almost as though God is crying out to us, 'Will you trust me? Please trust me' and yet we carry on our own sweet way.

We so need to be converted to the ways of God and understand love and its nature. We so need to be counter cultural in the way we live: trusting, believing, allowing God to be God. You see, there is always hope with God; always. The Scriptures face us time and time again with our own reality but they never leave us there. We forget it so easily when we become weighed down by the cares of our lives. God is a God of possibility and hope and new beginnings, a God of love. Ezekiel is sent to the Israelites with the word of God and for Ezekiel it all comes down to the one message, 'for I want to take hold of Israel's heart, the heart of all those who have strayed from me' (Ezek. 14:5).

You can almost hear the pain of God, a pain born of love. All God desires is that we give our hearts, that we allow God to be our lover, that we trust God. Unfortunately, we let our eyes be clouded by pettiness. We let worries ensnare and drag the life out of us. We trust in our own ways and in our own power. We jealously guard our heart and refuse to let God in. We hold on to our pain and our pettiness rather than let God be the Lord. Then, through the imagery of marriage, the people of Israel are reminded about the covenant with God and their abuse of it. It is the age-old message we find throughout the Prophets; God's faithfulness and Israel's unfaithfulness. Ezekiel knows the heart of God; love and life are central to who God is.

The message of The Book of Jonah can be divided into three parts. The first part is obedience to the word and the lesson that the wild storm teaches us. The second part is the lesson of the great whale and the paradox of the belly of the whale. The third part is compassion without limit, even for those who live on the edges, and the lesson that the castor oil plant teaches both Jonah and us. Jonah is brought to realise that God can show kindness to whom God wills, no matter which race or nation the people belong to, and even if they are living within the evil city of Nineveh.

Why should God show love and compassion to those on the outside? Why should God be merciful and forgiving towards people who in our eyes have done terrible things? Why is it that the scape-goating we all do, and the divide and conquer mentality that we all have is nothing in the face of God? Why does not God deal in black and white and right or wrong? Jonah becomes angry and depressed because his very image of God is being challenged, his very understanding of what makes life tick is being turned upside down, and it is too much for him to cope with. That God is unconditional love often turns us upside down because it turns on its head our need to have a vengeful God who deals with wicked people.

We are now going to look at the book of Isaiah. 1st Isaiah was written before the exile, about 750 BC, and runs from chapters 1-39. During the exile, another person in the school of Isaiah came along; some scholars think it might have been a woman. Whoever it was wrote the Book of Consolation, chapters 40-44. After the exile, another writer came along and they called that book 3rd Isaiah, chapters 45–66.

Isaiah is the great Prophet of faith. During his time there were a lot of wars and the great temptation for the kingdoms was to form alliances with Egypt, or Syria, or Assyria. Each time the people are tempted the Prophet says No; trust in God's love. He is amazingly politically involved which makes me smile at those who say the church should not be involved in politics. Isaiah speaks into the contemporary situation. He assesses the political situation and has something to say if you read chapter 1:2 and the people do not like it.

One of the major themes in Isaiah's writing is that of 'father-hood'. Isaiah sees that the father and judge become one. In Jewish courts, a father could never be the judge for his child; he was considered to be too biased. Isaiah says that your father in heaven is also your judge. He says, 'you have nothing to fear because he will judge you as a loving father; 'this is his domain in a peace that has no end, for the throne of David and for his royal power, establishes and makes secure, from this time and forever, the jealous love of Yahweh will do this.' Isaiah is becoming aware of the extraordinary nature of the love that is in the heart of God.

Isaiah also becomes filled with the concept of 'forever'. Up to this point in their history, the Jewish people have not been filled with the theme of 'forever'. For the Jew, time is now, life when it ends, ends; but Isaiah has experienced a 'forever father' who has an overwhelming and everlasting love for humanity. It is amazing how often 'everlasting' and 'forever' are used in Isaiah. It is as though the Prophet has experienced something deep down that is so real that he has to say, 'if this is not forever, then nothing is forever'. It is a new breakthrough in consciousness, to imagine the love that could be forever.

Whoever wrote 2nd Isaiah is a disciple of 1st Isaiah. The book was written around 500 BC at the end of the exile in Babylon where the Jewish people have been for 70 years. It's sometimes known as the Book of Consolation because it was trying to give people hope in a seemingly hopeless situation.

2nd Isaiah has the courage to stand up in the midst of despair and say, 'God is about to console us'. 'Console my people says the heart of God, speak to Jerusalem and call to her that her time of service is ended, her sin is atoned for, she has received from the Lord double punishment for her sins'.

The Israelites thought that everything came from God, even

punishment. The people did not realise that their actions had consequences and that what happened to them was a natural response to their lack of trust in Yahweh. They could only see that, had they trusted in Yahweh, things would have been different. In the Book of Consolation, the Prophet says that God will save his people so they begin to turn back to Yahweh and once again become his servants. They begin to see in their suffering, the hand of God teaching and leading and not punishing. There are four beautiful servant songs that express this. Israel is to be the suffering servant. The word we translate as servant is 'pi-es' which means 'boy', the boy of God. He is the boy of the father who gives his life in loving service to the father. Israel has to become the boy of God. Centuries later, Christians would take these songs of the suffering servants and see in them the presence of Christ. In the passion of Jesus, the words of the Prophet were ultimately fulfilled. Jesus becomes that boy and voluntarily, freely, with whole heart, becomes the boy of God and bears in his body the pain of God for the life of the world; to reveal this amazing love that has no beginning and no end but has always been, because God has always been. Isaiah describes the heart of God as his revelation unfolds. Somehow, the Prophet experiences in his own heart compassion and care which comes from something beyond him. Isaiah knows that it must be a reflection of what God's heart is. I love the quotation that says, 'Did you not know, Yahweh is an everlasting God, he created the boundaries of the earth, he does not grow weary'. God never loses hope in God's people and the love in God's heart is inexhaustible, never coming to an end. Where is this impossible hope coming from? Where is this understanding and compassion coming from? It must be from the very nature of God. It must be how God is. As the Prophet writes, 'he gives strength to the weary, he strengthens the powerless. Young men grow tired and weary but those who hope will never grow weary.'

There are lots of other prophets in the Bible. Some of them appear in stories like Elijah and Elisha and are known as non-writing prophets. Others have books named after them because their prophecies are written in the first person, and they are known as the writing prophets. Generally their message is the same. They have discovered a love that is outrageous and which nothing can deflect or destroy. That is the overriding theme of the prophets and yes, there may be passages that are trouble-some and worrying, but sometimes we just have to let them go as part of the human journey through which the spirit leads us to a wonderful revelation of love.

EIGHT

THE CROSS - THE GREATEST SIGN OF LOVE

I WAS WALKING ALONG THE PROMENADE IN LLANDUDNO recently. I was probably the youngest person there, but it is a place I love because I have many childhood memories of the North Wales coast, so I sometimes visit for a couple of days. As I walked along looking at the sea and minding my own business, I became aware of a man pushing a woman in a wheelchair. As I passed them, I smiled and said, 'good morning' and went to go on my way. His response was surprising. 'Motor Neurone disease' he said, nodding towards the chair. No greeting or smile; just this barked out phrase. I stopped and looked at the woman in the chair who had a fixed smile on her face. Her husband, as he turned out be, began to tell me of their lives. Without an ounce of self-pity he told the story of a daily struggle, the difficulties she had, his own battles and the caring that went on day by day. I sensed a need in the man and so suggested we find somewhere for morning coffee. He seemed delighted and continued the conversation as we went and found somewhere to sit. I sensed that this was a 'God moment', so when we settled, I waited until the stream of conversation came to an end. We sat in silence for some minutes and then he told me that he was a retired Baptist minister. At this point he did not know I was a priest. He had left his last parish under something of a cloud. He did not explain what the cloud was and told me he could not help the thought popping into his mind that somehow God was punishing him through his wife's illness.

I then told him I was a priest and the tears welled up in his eyes as he told me that he had been praying that morning for someone to help him. We went on to talk about images of God, and I said that in all of our lives, the passion, death and resurrection of Christ was being played out and, far from this illness being a punishment, it was a gift as both he and his wife are drawn closer into the mystery of Christ. He left me, I hope, seeing in his wife's illness the presence of the crucified Christ.

Reflecting on that encounter I realised again that on Good Friday, we do not just celebrate a 2000-year-old story. We celebrate every moment when we have died within, every moment of rejection and pain that we have experienced, every moment of isolation and disappointment, every hope and dream that has been crushed; and we see it all in the broken, bruised body of the Lamb hanging on the cross which is for us the greatest sign of the love of God.

Each Good Friday afternoon, we read from the Gospel of John. Do remember that the Gospels are very clever theological documents that are trying to help us discover the mystery of Christ. They are not biographies of Jesus. The Passion narrative begins with the arrest of Jesus. John has Jesus as a supremely free man; he is in control, and it is when he is ready that he allows the soldiers to take him from the garden.

The story tells us that a fracas breaks out between the disciples and those who come to arrest Jesus. In the fight, Peter cuts off the ear of the high priest's servant. The inclusion of this story reminds us that we cannot achieve God's ends by our means. It is a lesson that we have not really learnt. We constantly try to do our own thing, even when we are attempting to preach the Gospel. We have to go God's way; that is what brings life.

Jesus is taken before Annas and Caiaphas, the high priests, and Peter betrays Jesus three times, in front of a charcoal fire, to a young servant girl. Peter is going to have to go through the death of self before he can understand what Jesus is about, as we all do. It is interesting that Peter's response to his interrogation by the servant girl is the exact opposite of Jesus response to his questioning by Pilate Where Peter says, 'I am not' Jesus says, 'I am'.

Those two little words say a huge amount to us. The title, 'I Am' is reserved for God, and takes us back to the monologues in the Gospel where John has Jesus begin with that phrase to remind us who Jesus is. Unlike Peter, Jesus' 'I am' reveals the faithfulness of God. Jesus will be with the Church for all time, even when it appears that things are going wrong. He will not abandon or desert any one individual. We might believe he has gone but that is not reality. That is just our assumption, presuming that God acts as we do and walks away. The incarnation tells us that God never walks away, that God's colours are nailed to the mast.

We then find Jesus is taken before Pilate. The Roman trial has been placed at the centre of the Passion in John's Gospel so that we can see Jesus crowned as King even before he goes to the

Cross. The crowd has a choice between Barrabas and Jesus. Barrabas means Son of the father. Here we have the guilty son of the father being released instead of the innocent son of the father.

In Chapter nineteen, we find Pilate announcing Jesus to the world, 'Here is the man'. John is inviting us once again to understand at a deeper level. Pilate is not talking about Jesus but about the whole of humanity. Somehow this man, beaten, bleeding, about to be crucified, represents the whole of humanity. He represents you and me. Look at him and find yourself. In him you find your pain and your brokenness. In chapter one of the Gospel, John the Baptist announces Jesus to the world when he says, 'look there is the Lamb of God' It is as though John is saying, remember the Lamb of God. If this is his Kairos, his significant moment, then we too can find our Kairos in our suffering.

Many years ago, I met Fred Rose who was a priest in the Liverpool Archdiocese. Fred was a larger than life character who had a real passion for Jesus. He loved him with every fibre of his being. Fred had reached the bottom of the pit when alcohol took over his life. He ended up in a unit for priests who had difficulties. Fred said his shame knew no bounds; he had let everyone down, his parents, his sister and his friends and he did not know what to with himself. It was looking at the cross that saved Fred because as he looked at the cross, he began to see it was the way to life. If the cross of Jesus was his Kairos moment, then Fred began to see in his alcoholism and his shame his own significant moment. From here could come life, and that is what happened to Fred; he discovered a rich vibrant life that came from the depths of shame.

The Jews completely misunderstand what Jesus is about when they crown him with thorns. His way is not about glory and kingship. They have not understood. Mary as she was at Cana, is again the example of suffering humanity, suffering with God. She is the faithful one, simply trusting him, not because she understood but because she loved him. Her way is the way of the disciple; going with Jesus, dying to self, accepting and trusting. How willing are we to do that?

When Jesus says, 'I am thirsty' we have an echo of the conversation with the Samaritan woman reminding us again how God has chosen to need us. The guards respond with a sponge placed on a hyssop stick. This is a deliberate statement from John to remind us again of John the Baptist's statement early in the Gospel, 'Look there is the Lamb of God'. In the first Passover in Egypt, Moses ordered the hyssop stick to be used to sprinkle the blood of the lamb on the doorposts of those to be saved. John is reminding us, as Jesus dies, that his blood has set us free. Then we find that it is over. Once again, Jesus is in complete control of the situation and dies when he is ready and bowing gave up his Spirit.

This is John's Pentecost scene. He pours forth his Spirit on the new community being born through his death. His Spirit is yielded up to those who he loves and who are represented by the faithful ones at the foot of the cross - Mary, John, and Mary of Magdala. He is gone, but his spirit is present for the life of the world. It is interesting that this new community is born at the foot of the cross, the place where hostility and enmity are brought to an end. To be part of the church, as John understands it, is to recognise that there is no room for hostility, no room for scapegoating, or blaming another person. There is no room for accusing people or expelling people. All are welcome in the community that has its origin in the scandal of the cross, the instrument of torture that brings an end to the divisions that we as humans bring into the world. Desmond Tutu once said, 'when we see others as the enemy, we risk becoming what we hate. When we oppress others, we end up oppressing ourselves. All of our humanity is dependent upon recognising the humanity in others.' John then tells us of the blood and water flowing from his side, a reminder that the love of Christ must continue to be poured out in the life of the community.

In the other Gospels, Jesus also speaks final words from the cross that John does not include but which reveal the extraordinary love of God. In Matthew's gospel, Jesus cries out, 'my God, my God why have you forsaken me?' I am told that when Mother Teresa's intimate memoirs were published, they showed a real struggle with doubt and anxiety about the presence of God. In the mess of life I think most of us struggle with faith when seeming tragedy hits us or we watch some natural disaster. Richard Rohr says, 'when Jesus called out, 'my God, my God, why have you forsaken me?' He himself had to face the darkness and absurdity of life. On the cross, Jesus' human mind had no reason

to believe that God was his father, that God loved him, or that
this death had any transformative, redemptive meaning. At this
moment, Jesus fully and totally fell into the hands of the living
God and that is called resurrection. This is the mystery of faith.'
Jesus' cry comes from Psalm 22, which was written during the
exile in Babylon when the People of Israel felt as though God
had abandoned them. When any Jew uttered the first line of a
Psalm, he was not only crying out that line but also praying the
whole of the Psalm; and while the despair and anguish are real,
Psalm 22 ends with a real note of hope. When I cannot feel that
God is present and I feel abandoned, will I fall into grace and
trust that God will catch me? The challenge is whether or not I
will trust in the God who, in Jesus, became one of us and who
entered into the human condition, one who loves and suffers
with us. Will I trust in Jesus who weeps with us and who laughs
with us? Will I trust in Jesus who suffered on Calvary and yet in
that suffering brought an end to death forever? Will I trust in the
Jesus who shared in abandonment and disillusion when he hung
on the cross? Faith never takes away the pain and the despair;
nor does it give us a shortcut through the emotional hurt; but
maybe, just maybe, it gives us hope to begin again and to face
life with bravery. 'My God, why have you forsaken me?' Jesus
is an icon of humanity crying out to God and yet somehow
willing to trust that God will be God. He hangs on the cross and
identifies with every moment of abandonment. Such love!

In Luke's Gospel the words that come out of Jesus' mouth are
extraordinary as he hangs on the cross: 'Father forgive them for
they do not know what they are doing.' Extraordinary words in

the situation he found himself in. Many years ago, I was at a conference and the man who was leading it said that the greatest sign of the Kingdom of God is forgiveness. So Luke has Jesus hanging on a tree and saying 'this is what I am about... forgiveness'. What incredible love. Whatever baggage we carry around, whether it be lack of forgiveness of ourselves, other people, God, or institutions like the Church or the state, God loves us and will always forgive us. We may not always feel loved. We may look around the world or at our own lives and say, how can God love us? The wisdom of the Scriptures and of generations of believers is that God is love. Timothy Radcliffe in his book, 'Seven Last Words' says, 'forgiveness is there waiting for us before we ever sin. It is the scandal of the Gospel that whatever we do, whoever we are, God will always forgive.' It is again incredible love shown from the cross. The invitation the Gospel gives us is to fall into the arms of the living, loving God knowing that you do not have to be perfect to be loved. It is all captured in those words from the cross 'Father forgive them, they do not know what they are doing.'

Again in Luke's Gospel, the author has Jesus cry out more extraordinary words, 'Father, into your hands I commend my spirit.' This is a wonderful moment of trust as Jesus gives everything back to the Father. He entrusts us all, with all our fears and hopes, back into God's hands. It is the supreme act of trusting love, and it flies in the face of the fear that threatens to overwhelm us. Fear is at the root of much of the violence in society and causes us to hate, to blame and to scapegoat. Currently, there's a huge amount of fear about because of Ukraine and

Russia and where that conflict might lead. We are fearful of disease and illness particularly at the moment because of Covid-19 and all that has happened over these last two years. Many are afraid for, and about, their children, about their jobs. We are all afraid about failure and ultimately about death.

We suffer from a deep insecurity which is almost a collapse of trust. It is odd, because in many ways we are far more protected and safe than any previous generation in human history, at least in the West. We have better medicine, safer transport; we are more protected from the climate; we have better social security. And yet we are more afraid. When Jesus hangs on the cross and says, 'Father into your hands, I commit my spirit' it is the final letting go of fear and the need to control our fear. There is no need to be afraid. God can be trusted. Fear has no more hold over us, not even the greatest fear we have, the fear of death. To enter into relationship with the Son and the Father is to enter into eternity. It is to be able to see, and for those who can see, not even death is an obstacle. It is all about trust again. When Jesus dies, the evangelists tell us that the sun and the moon are darkened, the tombs are opened, and the dead walk. This is the end of which prophets spoke. The worst that one can ever imagine has already happened. The world collapsed. It fell apart but then there was Easter Sunday. Jesus invites us not to be afraid but to trust in God. All that we dread happened to him on Good Friday, the day that the old world ended, and a new world began. We can live because of love in the eternity of Easter.

On that first Good Friday, two days before he rises from the dead, Jesus looks at a thief being crucified alongside him and says that today, the good thief will be with him in Paradise, another of those words from the cross. It is obvious that God has a different sense of time than we do. Everything for God is in the eternal now, which means that God forgives us even before we have sinned and loves us eternally. How is it possible to believe that God's love is so extraordinary that we are forgiven from the moment of creation? We would rather try and earn that forgiveness with our petty, puny attempts to make up to God for the things we do wrong. All God wants us to do is accept it and stop fighting it; all God wants us to do is realise that salvation does not depend on us, but on God. We are not worthy; we can never be worthy, so try not to get caught up with worthiness. All we can do is stand under the waterfall and say thank you. I think that maybe the man hanging next to Jesus got all of that, and is not surprised when Jesus promises to bring him into Paradise before he has even risen from the dead.

This is because God lives in the present moment. Timothy Radcliffe says, 'God's eternity breaks into our lives now. Eternity is not what happens at the end of time, after we are dead. Every time we love and forgive then we have put a foot into eternity, which is God's life. and that is why we can be joyful even on Good Friday, even in the face of suffering and death.' Luke never says that those crucified with Jesus are thieves, only that they are criminals. Yet he is a thief because he knows how to get hold of what is not his. He gets Paradise without paying for it and as such stands for all of us because that is exactly what happens to us. It really is outrageous love. We can be in God's presence with all our weakness and failure, like the good thief, and still God takes pleasure in our very existence and promises Paradise to us.

It is because God is fiercely in love with us with a passion and an intensity which is almost frightening. I guess that is why we run away from God so much; we cannot cope with the intensity. Maybe our prayer life is about opening up to that relationship so that we can hear the good news that we are promised Paradise today and always. That is the good news that we have to share with those who are broken hearted and weighed down by life. God delights in us and promises joy that knows no end as we are invited into Paradise.

On the cross we see the perfection of love and all that it means. The cross teaches us that God is not a bystander to the human condition, but God is in the midst of that human condition, with all its pain and sorrow. As Richard Rohr says, 'Jesus forever tells us that God is found wherever the pain is, which leaves God on both sides of every war, in sympathy with both the pain of the perpetrator and the pain of the victim, with the excluded, the tortured, the abandoned, and the oppressed since the beginning of time.'

I would like to look at Paul's understanding of this central truth within Christianity. Paul knew that we are already loved by God; we are already children of God; Jesus is the one who came back to reclaim his own. That could well be the real meaning of reconciliation and redemption which are words we use when speaking of the cross. The cross can be seen as a visual reaching out by God to those who already belong to God. The word 'justification' is also taken from the legal system. It is remarkably similar to our word 'acquittal'.

Having said all that, we can never really understand the extra-ordinary mystery of love that we are faced with in the image of the cross. Ronald Rolheiser says, 'precisely because it is such a deep mystery, the cross is not easy to grasp intellectually. The deeper things in life - love, fidelity, morality, and faith - are not mathematics, but mysteries whose unfathomable depths always leave room for more still to be understood. We never quite arrive at an adequate understanding of them.'

I think the cross is the greatest revelation of who God really is. This is pure, unconditional love, which is the heart and nature of God. All who follow Jesus believe that the cross is redemptive, that it saves us. You then get into another theological word, 'salvation'. What does that mean? Is it just about going to heaven when we die, or is it also about an experience of life now? Is it about being saved from our sins and from eternal punishment, or is it about a quality of life lived now and forever? Are we, in fact, saved from ourselves? John Ortberg, the famous Christian writer says, 'The good news, as Jesus preached it, is not just about the minimal entrance requirements for getting into heaven when you die. It is about the glorious redemption of human life, your life.' So, redemption seems to be a combination of all of that and more. God, captured in the person of Jesus, reveals

Godself to the world and, in that pouring out of sacrificial love, we are healed and freed to live life to the full here and now.

There are lots of theological attempts to explain the meaning of the cross. One of them is the substitution theory which for me is really not very helpful but which many Christians believe. I remember as a little boy crying because I was told my sins had put Jesus on the cross and he had taken my place. It conjures up images of God that any right reading of the Scriptures and of our tradition would make us recoil from. I hope that all I have shared so far helps us to see that God is not distant from humanity. Love overcomes distance. Nor is God cold, furious, or harshly punishing, exacting blood from Jesus so that every human being can experience freedom for all eternity. I cannot believe that the God I have met on so many occasions in the Scriptures, in the sacraments, in my brothers and sisters, demands retribution for our sins. Any study of God that arrives at the conclusion that God demands blood for sin is beyond my comprehension. I can understand that God used the cross to show us the truth of love, God's amazing, overwhelming love for the whole of humanity; and yes, God can turn all things to good as Paul tells us in the letter to the Romans. For me, to see the death of Jesus in any other way is repugnant because, from the very beginning of time, God has been and always will be; love. Ronald Rolheiser captures it very beautifully in a quotation I have used before when he writes, 'What Jesus' suffering on the cross reveals, among other things, is that real love costs and costs dearly. If we want sustained, faithful, and life-giving love in our lives, the kind of pain that Jesus suffered on the cross is its price tag.'

Jesus captures the reality of real love on the cross so that we might see it for all time and know the truth, that from the very moment of our creation, we are forgiven and loved and cherished. Dare we believe that to be true? Can we live our lives trusting in goodness and believing that everything will be redeemed, however broken and however painful?

NINE

PARABLES OF LOVE

WHEN I WAS IN THE SEMINARY, THERE WAS A STUDENT THERE named Eddie. Every morning after breakfast and before lectures started, lots of students would walk around the lake situated in front of the house. Sometimes those short walks were full of laughter, and other times there would be revelations that would break your heart. One day, while we were out walking, Eddie told us about something that moved me to tears. When he was six years old his mother, who sounded a very confused young woman, handed him over to social services. Standing on the steps of the building, he watched his tearful mother wave goodbye through the back window of a taxi. Eddie was frightened and angry, and I could hear the pain in his voice when he told me that he had broken free from the social worker holding his hand. He ran after the taxi shouting at the top of his lungs, 'Mummy, Mummy, please do not go'. That turned to cries of, 'I hate you! I hate you! I will never forgive you!'

Eddie was adopted and that turned out well for him. His adoptive family loved him and gave him everything they could; but still, he said, he felt he did not fit in, nor did he ever really feel that he belonged to his family. Eddie did not see his birth mother again for years and despite his gut feelings of pain and rejection; he never gave in and became one of those people who almost dance through life. Nothing ever seemed to get him down. Whatever troubles he had, he faced with gusto. He trained to become a teacher and worked with those who have special needs. In his spare time, he played football and was always the life and soul of the party. He eventually felt the call to train for priesthood. Despite it all, deep within, Eddie was haunted by his mother's rejection at that early age and it hung around his neck, weighing him down, and always causing him to think that he was less than he really was despite how popular and able he was.

Just before he came to the seminary, Eddie decided that he had to find his mum and lay to rest the nagging feelings that he had held throughout his life. He set out on his search. At first, he thought he would never find her, but one day, he got a phone call from a woman who knew his birth mother. She told him that, years earlier, she had worked with his natural mother and had a telephone number for one of her sisters. Through her, he eventually found where she was living and got a telephone number for her in New Zealand of all places. He decided to ring her. After all she had rejected him once; she could only do it again and he had to do something to lay this all to rest before training to be a priest. So, he telephoned his mother. She started to cry immediately he told her who he was, and Eddie said that he was filled with compassion and love for her. He stammered out, 'Mum, I love you and I forgive you.' After a long, sobbing telephone conversation, the longest chase in years was ended. For years Eddie had been chasing that taxi in his mind. Now it was finally over. At his ordination, Several years later, I was introduced to a slim nervous woman with a hint of a New

Zealand accent. Eddie's mum had finally come home. It was an experience of love and mercy that I have never forgotten.

Luke has several main themes running through his Gospel. It is primarily a missionary document because Luke's community is obviously concerned to spread the Good News. People are always being sent out.

That's a call which is still necessary today and to which people are still responding. It's obvious that new ways of proclaiming the Gospel have to be found because the old ways are done. Pope Francis has written 'I dream of a 'missionary option', that is, a missionary impulse capable of transforming everything, so that the Church's customs, ways of doing things, times and schedules, language and structures can be suitably channelled for the evangelisation of today's world rather than for her self-preservation.'

Luke's understanding is that it has to be the Gospel of inclusion, forgiveness, mercy and compassion that is spread. It is so sad that we as Church miss so many opportunities to be inclusive and merciful. Luke's perspective is much wider than either Matthew or Mark. By his time of writing, Christians have made the break with Judaism and have begun to see themselves as something different. Luke is not afraid of offending the Jewish Christians. He is a little like a convert to Catholicism who does not have the same hang ups that the rest of us have. Luke is the most broad-minded and the most forgiving of the evangelists. Every chance he gets, Luke has Jesus forgiving people, right up to the good thief on the cross. It pervades almost every story he tells. There seems to be no limit to God's mercy; all are called to salvation, the poor, social outcasts, the gentiles. Inclusivity again!

So with that background, we find, right at the centre of Luke's Gospel, three parables which for me capture the essence of Luke's understanding of the nature of God. Luke begins his series of three with the parable of the sheep and the Shepherd. Shepherds normally counted their sheep at the end of the day to make sure all were accounted for.   I have read that sheep naturally are very social, and that an isolated sheep can quickly become bewildered, and even neurotic. So, the shepherd would have been anxious about the sheep that was missing and, even though it was mad to do so, goes searching for that sheep at night when anything could have happened. The shepherd takes a risk. Our God takes risks to search for us. God took a risk in Jesus to search for us. It is part of the nature of God.

The shepherd's worry turns to joy when he finds the lost sheep and restores it to the fold. The compassion of the shepherd searching for the sheep is a very moving image. God is like the shepherd who leaves all his sheep to look for the lost one. It is craziness and it is risky. It makes no sense at all unless you are the one that is lost. It is about love that knows no boundaries, and which will go to the ends of the earth for the sake of those that are loved.

Many years ago, I was leading a retreat in an Augustinian house in the village where Dame Vera Lynn had made her home. Even though she was not a Catholic, she had become great friends with the sisters and was a frequent visitor to their house. On the day I was leaving, I was asked if I would like to meet her. Of course, I said yes and was taken to her house for morning coffee. When I arrived, I met a charming woman who was really very ordinary. We sat and chatted about her very interesting life, but it was never all about her. She wanted to know about what I did and why I did it. When she began talking about the war, I told her how grateful my dad had been to her during the second world war because she enabled him to keep in touch with a little bit of normality through her songs and radio shows. Her eyes filled up when I said that, but when it got to the stories of Burma and her trips out the troops, she really began to cry. She told me that she had been terrified to go because it was so dangerous out there. The thought of being captured by the Japanese sent her legs to jelly. Once there, she knew she had to stay for the sake of 'her boys'. Then she said something that made a shiver go down my spine. She said that it was all about a deep love that she had for those men who were willing to give everything for the sake of truth and justice. She told me that she did not know them, but she loved them. She was saying something so very important; it was all about love. It gave me another insight into the reality of God, and I doubt that Dame Vera knew that she had done that for me.

These parables of love and mercy must have been a real challenge to the Scribes and Pharisees whose image of God is of one who rejects the sinner, while Jesus tries to show them that

God is there for those whose lives are a mess. Shepherds were unclean and lived on the edges. It is no wonder the Scribes and Pharisees hated Jesus. He challenged even their image and understanding of God, and in doing so threatened the very fabric of Jewish society. I often wonder whether things are so different today. Much of the antagonism against Pope Francis comes from the Scribes and Pharisees of our day, those who are unwilling to allow God to be a God that sets people free, a God of mercy and compassion. Those who would rather keep God as small and petty and unwilling to bend are always reacting to the God of unconditional love. I do not know what your image of God is like, but I certainly do not believe in a God who waits for us to say 'sorry' before pouring out forgiveness. I do not believe in a God who waits for us to try and get our lives together before meeting us in our need. I believe in a God whose essence is loving mercy.

I cannot really begin to put words on it. It is too big for me. It is too great for me. It is such good news. Why are we unable to believe in this amazing love? Why are we so afraid of it and find it so difficult to cope with? Why do we limit it and put conditions on it? Why do we think it is about our being good and moral and upstanding? It is a free gift, and it is given for you and me. It is an extraordinary reality.

Then Luke tells us this God is like the woman who lost a drachma. Women were of little value in Jewish society and yet, like the shepherd, this woman becomes an image of the God of loving mercy. God will search for us, as she searches for the coin, until we are found, so that we can begin to know the truth that we are loved. The housewife who lost a coin faced an economic disaster because the value of the coin would be equivalent to her husband's daily wage. Her worry and anxiety turn to joy when she finds the coin. Again, like the story of the shepherd, it is nonsense. The party the woman held once she found the coin would have cost more than the money that was lost.

Luke is trying to tell us that God is completely other than we are. He is trying to get a handle on the ferocious, overwhelming love that is the heart of God, and which is focused on you and me. Both the shepherd and the housewife 'search until what they have lost is found'. Their persistence pays off. God searches for us even in the midst of our sin, our brokenness, our pain. God is always reaching out for us. That is what Jesus came to reveal to us. Love is seeking us out and we do not have to be any particular shape to be met by love. Love is simply searching, and will search till the end of time. It is all about love. If you and I have been found by God, then our response has to be gratitude. How grateful are we? If we have been found by God, then we are invited to join in searching out whoever is lost.

Finally, we have the famous story of the Prodigal Son. Certainly, the story Jesus tells of the Prodigal Son is an invitation to face ourselves because all three characters are there within us and we can choose who we want to be. Luke's Gospel always gives us choices: The Pharisee and the Publican, the widow and the judge. This parable too gives us choices.

We can be like the first Son, with all his headstrong opinions, need to fulfil himself and to go his own way at the expense of his relationships and his life. He returns knowing his need for mercy and forgiveness. He knows he does not deserve it, nor does he really expect it as he begins to stammer out his words of sorrow. How foolish he must have felt when the father is not even prepared to listen but is already pushing the ring on his finger and letting the servants clothe him, ready for a banquet. I guess all he can do is rejoice in the love he experiences. I know that in me is the wayward younger brother, and I am sure he lies within you too.

We can be like the second son, full of resentment and anger at what happens to his brother. I think many of us are like this young man, murmuring about others and what they do or do not do, angry at others for their waywardness, and so avoiding hearing the truth of God's love and mercy for all, even the faithful. If I am honest, the self-righteous elder son in me raises his head far more than the others do. He hides behind words and phrases like 'in MY opinion' or 'do you not think' or 'is it not dreadful to live like that' or, 'is it not wrong to do that'. He hides behind the moral high ground that so many of us take, and the judging and condemning we indulge in. At his worst extreme, he believes that only he is right; and we only have to look at our T.V. screens to see where that leads time and again.

Because of his attitude, the second son misses out on the celebration. For those who spend their lives in bitterness and anger, there is no celebration in life. For those who live focused on mercy, forgiveness and love there are lots of celebration. We can accept and rejoice in God's forgiveness and love, or live life consumed by bitterness and anger and refuse to recognise the love and the mercy of God. Which son do you want to be?

I know within me too is the compassionate welcoming father. In those moments when we do not judge others and do not condemn them, in those times when we stretch out our hands to help others, in those moments when we are filled with compassion, we experience that power which is the father. The more time we spend allowing the father to grow within us, the more life we experience within ourselves and can share with others.

More than that, the character of the father reveals the nature of God. I recently read that in the Palestine of Jesus' time, for a son to treat his father in the way the younger son had treated the father was a crime punishable by stoning, should the son ever return to the village. The only salvation would have been the father's acceptance of the son. The restoration of the son would have shown the villagers that the father had forgiven the son and loved him. Is it any wonder that the father in the story is always looking for his son? It is a matter of life and death that the father should be the first to meet the son and show the villagers that he has been re-instated; hence the ring, the best robe and the feast.

What is Luke telling us? Luke is telling us that God is love and will go to any lengths to find the person who is lost; that God would risk Godself for the sake of us collectively and for me individually; that there is no need to be afraid of what God might do in the face of our messy and broken lives; that God is love and will only love. As if to reinforce that message Luke tells us that when the lost are found there will be celebration: the shepherd with the sheep, the woman with her coin, and the father with his son.

That love is the Good News. Love is the name of God. It is what religious practice is all about, what two thousand years of tradition have been about. The forgiveness and mercy of God made flesh in Jesus, the unconditional love that knows no bounds are the nature of God. No wonder the tax collectors and sinners were all seeking his company. With a message like that who would not seek him? It promises life and peace. And yet, even those of us who say we love God and follow Jesus do not always take it to heart. We hope that it is true, we want it to be true and yet at the same time so many of us live our lives afraid of judgement and condemnation. I think it is because we judge God's love by the standards of human love, which is always conditional. Thank God that God is not contained by human definition. God is love; pure, perfect love.

If only our image of God was of one who seeks out what was lost and rejoices in it. If only we would only believe that God is like that for us and for others. If only we could believe that God wants to heal us of anything that makes us feel lost or alienated whether it be fear, depression, anxiety, past hurts or anything else, so that we can find our true selves and rejoice in that self.

I think it is for our sake and not for God's sake that God wants to deal with the sin that helps us lose sight of who we are. The father in the story deals with the son's sinfulness by loving him. I think it is a common misconception that our sin offends God because God is good and so as not to offend God's goodness, we need forgiveness. Our sin affects God because it damages us, and all God wants, because of God's outrageous love, is our wholeness and health. God looks at us with mercy and compassion and will go to any lengths to find us in our times of being lost; and we all have them.

If we believed in unconditional love, then maybe we would see things like guilt in a very different way, and would learn to trust in God so that we would not live frightened to death of every action that we do in case it is a sin. Maybe we would begin to believe that God loves us enough to treat us with mercy and compassion and to rejoice in us when we are found.

I was once accused of arrogance for believing in the love of God, but I know that I would rather live believing in love, mercy and compassion than in any other image of God. God loves the whole of humanity, collectively and singularly, and life would be so different if we could only really accept that love and allow it to flow through us into the world. If we believed in the love and mercy of God for ourselves, then maybe we would begin to believe in it for others. It is then we would know there is no room for judgement and condemnation of others' lifestyles, and what others do or do not do because God, in the love and mercy that flows from the heart of God has not condemned us. Maybe our knowledge of the God who seeks out the lost would force us to have compassion on those who feel alienated and lost, and on those who live on the fringes of society. Maybe we would begin to identify with the needs of those who do not have a handle on life and walk with them. Perhaps we would begin to understand the truth of the wonder of humanity. Maybe we would begin to understand that when you touch another person, you are touching God and when another person is touching you, they are touching God. I came across this quotation from Richard Rohr recently, 'when there is an encounter with another, when there is mutuality, when there is presence, when there is giving and receiving, and both are changed in that encounter that is the moment when you can begin to move toward transformation. Do not let the word transformation scare you. You just allow what you have met to change you. You look back at it with different eyes. Now you are able to look at the rest of your life with different eyes.'

Love transforms you. It changes you within. Encounters with unconditional love always set you free and bring you new life. Kathleen and John were a lovely couple I met in the Vauxhall area of Liverpool. They lived in a block of flats just opposite the church in their city centre parish. Kathleen was a sweet gentle soul and John was a larger than life character who had made his money on the docks but never wanted to leave the area he had grown up in. They were kindness itself, but when John took me out for a drink one night, he told me that it had not always been like that. In the 1950s, John had been a real wide boy. He worked on the docks with an eye for the main chance and the quick deal, legal or otherwise, was never far away from him. He spent his evenings and weekends drinking in the clubs and pubs of Liverpool. He was always getting into fights and said that if he had not met Kathleen, he did not know where he might have ended up. At first, she would not go anywhere near him because of his reputation; but John, with his huge personality, would not give up and pursued her. He had fallen head over heels in love with her. She eventually went out with him but as they began to get serious, Kathleen told John that if he wanted a future with her, then his stealing from the docks, his carousing each night and the fighting all had to stop. John looked at me with his steely blue eyes and said, 'so it stopped, all of it, from that day onwards'. They got married, had a family, and John returned to the church. Kathleen's love had transformed this bear of a man into a wonderfully warm human being who spent his life looking after Kathleen and his family and then helping anyone around them who needed help. Again, his story spoke me to me of God's love and the way in which it can transform us if we allow it to.

There are many other parables of love that we could have reflected on: the story of the good Samaritan which reveals the face of God to us; the parable of the landowner who pays all his workers the same amount however long they have worked; the list goes on. I have picked three that Luke puts together to form a unit in his Gospel. Whichever I had picked, they all tell us something very clearly: that the name of God is love.

TEN

LOVE RECEIVED AND SHARED

NORAH WAS AN ELDERLY WOMAN I MET IN THE VAUXHALL district of Liverpool when I was serving there as a deacon. In her late seventies, she was the sort of woman who could easily fade into the background. She was, seemingly, insignificant. I met her most days at Mass but apart from a beaming smile and a quick hello, I did not get to know her at all. So, one day, I decided to call and see her. She lived in a council flat about five minutes from the church. She had her coat on when I arrived and explained that she had just come in from the mother and toddler group that ran in the area.

Norah went into her tiny kitchen to make coffee and I sat and waited for her. When she finally joined me, she seemed a little nervous, maybe wondering why I was there. I got the feeling that she was not used to talking about herself, but after a while she began to warm up and shared some of her story. Like many people in Vauxhall, she had been born there at the beginning of the 20th century and lived within a square mile all her life. She was the youngest of nine, born into abject poverty. She and her family lived in one of Liverpool famous courts and she used to beg in Scotland Road's famous markets.

The courts were groups of tall, narrow, terraced houses. They often had as many as twelve or fifteen families living together in each one. Each family would live in one or, at the most, two rooms. They were built around a courtyard, hence the name. In the courtyard was the one toilet that everybody in the court shared. The houses were usually in a terrible condition, damp and dirty with rags shoved into holes in the windows to stop the penetrating damp. Illnesses caused by the condition were rampant and rats and mice were children's playthings. It was a dreadful way to have to live, but Norah smiled as she shared her family life and the love and faith that held them together. Eventually the courts were demolished and Norah, who was the only one of the children left at home, moved into a tenement block with her parents. At least here they were not as cramped and had an inside toilet. The tenements were eventually demolished and Norah, by herself now, was rehoused in the flat that I was sitting in. She seemed to have very few needs and was content in her life. When I asked what she did, she was a bit reticent to tell me. Mass was the centre of the day and after that she said she helped out at a few things. I left Norah, glad to have given her the chance to reminisce and to talk and thought no more of it.

As I got more used to the area, I began to visit several community projects, food banks, nursery's, credit unions, pensioners clubs and wherever I went, I met Norah. These were the 'few things' that Norah 'helped out' at. I discovered she was one of the main people behind the credit union. She had founded the mother and toddler group and the pensioners group. She was on the committee for the famous Eldonian Village. In her quiet, deprecating way she had not really wanted me to know what she did in case I thought she was blowing her own trumpet.

One day I was in the mother and toddler group and Norah was on the floor with a couple of babies crawling over her. I sat down next to one of the mums who was at pains to tell me that she did not really believe in God. Then her eyes filled up and she nodded at Norah and said to me, 'but if I did I would find God in that woman.'

You see, the face of God can be found in the most ordinary of people. These people may well have had an ignominious start in life. They may well have nothing much to show for their years on earth other than and this is everything, a depth of compassion and love which has its roots in God. Our lives, if we want them to, can be a revelation of the mystery of Christ and the love he pours out on the world.

Just recently, I led a course reflecting on the book of Colossians, which for me is all about the revelation of love for us in the heart of God. In declaring that love, the author claims that we are made in the image and likeness of love. So we become vessels of this love that is God, allowing it to flow through us into a broken needy world.

I think it is fair to say that we know very little about the letter to the Colossians. We do not really know when it was written or who the Colossians were. We do not know what happened to give rise to the letter or much about the society in which its author lived. The scholars are fairly certain that it was not written directly by Paul, although some would say there is a slight possibility that he might have had something to do with its writing; and if he did then it was probably written while he was in prison in Ephesus, but it really is unlikely. It is more probable that it was written by someone from the Pauline tradition who wanted to use Paul's authority to give the letter more credence in the eyes of the Colossians.

Colossians is very different to any of the other letters to the early Christian communities because the letter does not limit itself to seeing the local church as being an entity in itself, or even as its members being citizens of a political system which is bigger than the community. It uses as its backdrop the whole of the universe. The author of Colossians sees Jesus, the Christ, as the key with which the meaning of the universe as a whole is unlocked. What you discover is that the meaning of the universe is love. Love underpins everything and holds all things together. What this letter tries to say to us is that this Christ is bigger and more than we can ever imagine. Love is bigger and more than we can imagine. How on earth we can put the petty limitations on Christ that we do, I have no idea. How can we say that we know him or understand the ways that he works? I think we can experience his presence in our lives but to know him is impossible.

We try and rationalise what is beyond rationale, making God into something we can handle, putting God into a box that is manageable and neat when the truth is that God's love is so far beyond anything we can understand. It is not respectable and nice but radically transformative because it is the foundation stone of the universe, and as such, it cannot be contained.

Accepting that love is not about becoming more religious or more pious or more devotional. It is about being open to a power that can, if you let it, turn your life upside down so that you become a different person, more loving, more compassionate and ripped apart by the pain of the world. Radical love changes you if you want it to change you. I am never sure how many of us who say we follow Christ really want that change. We are happy to be nice but not transformed. In order to experience love and the transformation it leads to, the I, the great big I, has to somehow get out of the way and let God happen within. Even our images of God, our practice of religion, can be about the ego; that is why opening to transformative love is always about going to that place of nothingness, facing ourselves and letting go in order to find a deeper reality. Rob Bell, the evangelical preacher, says that our relationship with God, 'is trusting that I am loved, that I always have been, that I always will be. I do not have to do anything. I do not have to prove anything, or achieve anything, or accomplish one more thing. That, exactly as I am, I am totally accepted, forgiven, and there is nothing I could ever do to lose this acceptance.'

I remember meeting a woman in a retreat centre who told me she was a recovering alcoholic. I can only tell you that she sparkled in the way that people who have been given a second chance of life, sparkle. She described her life with a self deprecating humour that was infectious, while never denying the truth of her trauma. She had been married three times and had six children, none of whom spoke to her because of the way she had treated them down the years. She described the lies she had told, the one night stands she had had. She said the low point in her life was when she ended up on the streets drinking cheap cider. What made the difference? She stumbled into a church one night and heard the preacher telling the truth that there was nothing that could separate us from the love of God. It made her think. She went back to her squat and poured away the cider she had hidden. She fell off the wagon several times but the spirit had worked within her and she knew the truth that she was loved, accepted and forgiven and so she battled on, finally putting her life back together until she had become this wonderfully rounded, sparkling human being that I had met.

In the first chapter of the letter to the Colossians, there is a famous hymn of praise to Jesus which describes his nature in terms of the very structure of reality. You know, the very fabric of creation is imbued with the presence of this loving God. The image of God is in every tiny leaf and every creature that exists. Those things are not God, but they bear something of the image of God and so should be treated with the utmost care, if only we could see. St Bonaventure, who is a doctor of the Church, wrote that he saw the 'traces' or 'footprints' of God in all things. He said that the whole world was the 'incarnation' of the mystery of God, and the very 'Body of God.' The 'journey of the mind to God,' as Bonaventure put it, was to learn how to see the unity of all being, how to listen for the partially hidden God, and how to honour the footprints that were everywhere once you could see. If only we could recognise that God is everywhere; we would crawl around this world on our knees, aware of our own smallness in the face of God, of our own incredible dignity as bearers of the divine imprint, and the gift that is the whole of the created order.

I often think of the words that Nelson Mandela used in his inauguration speech when he challenged the listeners to recognise their own dignity as children of God. We do not have the right to walk around with a poor self-image, thinking how bad we are. God lives in us. Love is within us. When are we going to realise it? I sometimes think we need a revolution within us to shift us out of our preoccupation with ourselves and how bad we are, so that we can proclaim the truth of a God who is everywhere and in everything. I find it very sad that we sometimes look at this world with all its beauty and say that God is in some things and not in others. It is extraordinary that we, with all our human limitations, can look and decide where God is and how God works. How do we have the temerity to think that we, who are on this earth for such a short time, can ever second-guess where God is and how God works? God is in the most extraordinary places as well as our churches and our faith communities, and is always bigger and more than we expect.

So, the letter begins with a prayer where the reader is encouraged to be grateful for all that God has done and is doing. It is almost as though the author is saying to us, if you are entering into a relationship with God, then you will be beginning to open up to the truth that this God of love is more on your side than you are yourself, and all you can be is grateful. It is almost as though gratitude has to be at the very core of who we are, and if we are not grateful then we have not understood who Christ is and what we are called to.

The other day I opened up an old Pastoral review magazine to see the title of an article 'Gratitude a one word summary of the Catholic faith' and I remembered something that I read by Ronald Rolheiser, who said that only the grateful heart is the transformed heart. I then thought about an old lady that I met in Blackpool a couple of years ago who said that for sixty years she had practiced gratitude every day. I began to then ask myself the questions do I have a grateful heart? Am I grateful for the gift of life? Am I grateful for the people around me? Am I grateful for the air that I breathe, the creation that I live in? Am I grateful for the good and the bad that comes in life because of what it can teach me? Or is my life soured by negativity and disappointment? Am I always dissatisfied and critical? Is the world a bad place to be endured? Do I treat people badly? Do I only think of myself? Do I reject and push away those that I find difficult? Those questions are the signs of a heart that needs to be more open to transformation and so I guess we all need transformation. Transformation is at the heart of the Gospel and if we are followers of Jesus we have to be about what he was about. Faith is not just about going to Church; anybody can go to Church. Faith is about relationship that transforms the heart so that it becomes the grateful heart that is a sign of the Kingdom of God. The grateful heart is the heart that has been touched by the Gospel.

The scholars think that Colossians 1:15-20 is probably a fragment of a prayer or song used by Christians of the first century in their worship and inserted into the letter because it expressed the kind of faith needed by the community in its time of crisis. The predominant theme of the hymn is very clear: the Christ in whom the Colossians must believe is the foundation of all existence, and the primary link between the world and God who is both creator and redeemer. It reminds us, slightly, of the prologue of John's Gospel.

Colossians 1: 15-20 is a pivotal point from which to explore the message of the letter as a whole. The hymn presents, in beautifully evocative language, the truth that the whole letter proclaims. That is why the author begins by reminding us that in Christ, we have the image of the invisible God. That is a huge statement to make about Jesus. You know, we have years of tradition, and that phrase almost rolls glibly off the tongue. What does it really say about the love of God who was willing to become human with all the human limitations to show us just how much we are loved? It is amazing, and for the author of the letter to say it is even more amazing, because at the time the letter was written, the early Church was struggling to grasp who Jesus is, and how he could be the God who had long been revealing Godself to humankind through his chosen people, the Jews.

For most Christians at the time the letter was written, the way God had revealed Godself was in the Old or First Testament. The first way that the relationship between Jesus Christ and the God of the Old Testament was expressed by the earliest Christians was with the imagery of 'Father and Son.' In Colossians 1:3, God is called 'the Father of our Lord Jesus Christ'. Jesus is called the 'beloved Son' in Colossians 1:13. It is the earliest and most fundamental way of expressing the relationship between Jesus and the God of Israel. If only we could come to terms with what that means. I know, because of the father wound in my own life, that the father/child image has difficulties for many people but in Jewish understanding it had particular meaning; the Son was loved by the father and everything the father had would be given to the son. You and I are loved by God, and everything God is has been given to us in Jesus. Again, as I have said before, it really is mind blowing.

Yet so many of us seem unable to let the reality of love in. One Saturday morning, I was in a local prison leading a morning of mercy. We began with Mass because the lads had only had Mass two or three times during lockdown and then we had a time of reflection and groups and a question and answer session. At the end, there was a cup of tea and during the social time a young guy called James came and sat with me. He told me that this was his first time in prison and he was terrified. I do not know what he had done but it cannot have been that bad because he was only serving two years and he was due for parole fairly soon. During the session, I had read the Gospel story from John's Gospel, about the woman taken in adultery. James was crying when he told me that he really identified with that woman. He said that he had been dragged before the courts; his shame had been laid bare before everyone and he knew that at home, fingers were being pointed at his wife and his mum and dad because of what he had done. He continued to cry as he told me that he had a real difficulty in forgiving himself and, more than that, accepting God could forgive him. He had bought the lie that God is merely an extension of our own petty need to condemn and punish others for what they do. It is so sad that we cannot simply fall into grace and let God be God for us, which would free us and transform us. We are children of God and all that means to the author of the letter to the Colossians. We are loved by God.

Instead of discussing the sonship of Jesus Christ further, the author of Colossians decides to reflect on 'image' to express the nature of Christ and, through him, the nature of everything that is, ever has been and ever will be. In the ancient world, philosophically as well as in the Old or First Testament, the word 'image' was associated with the origin, nature, or creation of the world. To use the word at all acts as a reminder of the story of the creation of the first human beings that is told in the early chapters of the Book of Genesis. The author of that book is obviously telling us that humankind was created by God and that this creation was accomplished 'in God's image.' In some of the theological books, the scholars said that could mean that the first man and woman were created according to a kind of divine pattern, 'God's image.' Or it could mean that they were created as two parts of a whole, itself an image of God.

I guess what it says more than anything else, yet again, is that God is love. We cannot escape that truth which leaps out of the pages of these ancient books. However the world was created, God is the loving author. The ancient writers want us to know that every aspect of creation is gift, all of it finds its substance because of the grace of God. Everything comes from the goodness of God who, time and again in the scriptures, makes something out of nothing. Creation itself is an illustration of the process of something coming from nothing; the forming of a child in a virginal womb, centuries later, is another reminder. God creates, and all of that creation is good and to be enjoyed. It is all about love. When the author says in Colossians 1:15 that 'Christ is the image of the invisible God,' all of that understanding of love comes into play. If Jesus is the image of the unseen God, then he is love as God is love.

For the ancient people of Israel, God was revealed to be not only a God who entered into human lives and the events of human history, but also to be a God who was mysterious, and who totally transcended human understanding, increasingly aloof from the world. As they went through the wars and captivities that marred their history, God seemed remarkably aloof from them. As the 'image' of the invisible and transcendent God, Jesus made the inaccessible God suddenly accessible in the world instead of far away. As image, Jesus shares in the divine nature, because in the philosophy of the time, an image had a share in the reality of the original. The Father is invisible, but the beloved Son, as image, is visible. The Christ of Colossians is God himself in visible form. Christ is still God touching our lives and holding our world together, however much it seems to be tearing itself apart. We too, as sharers in the image of God, are making real the face of God. We who are created out of love are to love in the way revealed to us by Jesus, the cosmic Christ. The cosmic Christ is a view of Christology which emphasises the extent of Jesus Christ's concern for the cosmos. The biblical bases for a cosmic

Christology is often found in Colossians, Ephesians, and the prologue to the gospel of John. To say that we believe in the cosmic Christ means that we are invited to make a positive choice to live in a particular way. It is a choice to live believing in potential, possibility, hope and goodness. It is to live in the world with a heart and mind that is unlocked and available. To choose to love as Jesus loved means there is no room in our hearts for hatred and mistrust, judgement and condemnation.

It is not an emotional reaction to the world and its people, but a choice as to how we view the world and how we act. It is a way of encompassing the world rather than remaining apart from it. To love like Jesus means you reach out to those that the world rejects: the person of colour, the addict, the gay people, the street people, those with mental health issues. Love for most of us is seen as an emotion or a feeling. The love of the Gospels that permeates every encounter and every story in the Gospels is not about feelings; it is a stance or a position that we choose. It is not a theory; it insists that we make the choice to reach out to those in our society who experience rejection from others and the judgement of others. It is not an easy way of living, but it is the call of those who follow Christ to, like him, reveal the image of the unseen God.

ELEVEN

WHAT CAN SEPARATE US FROM THE LOVE OF GOD?

SOME MONTHS AGO, A FRIEND OF MINE WHO HAS MENTAL health issues invited me to a concert at the Liverpool Philharmonic Hall. The event was being hosted by an organisation called Life Rooms which provides a safe place for people with mental health issues to gather, and along with others, to do various courses that will enhance mental health.

My friend, Nicky, has benefitted a great deal from Life Rooms and the courses offered there. Nicky was taking part in this concert and wanted her mum, me and a few friends to go. I was not prepared for the emotional roller coaster that happened within me as I watched these extraordinary human beings share deeply, not only about their issues, but also about their giftedness. The first half of the concert was a musical rendition of songs that had helped people cope with their situations. The bravery they showed in getting up in front of an audience was moving enough; but the second half of the concert left me an emotional wreck. Each of the participants picked a song and then shared why that song meant so much to them. My friend Nicky used a Phil Collins song, 'Another day in Paradise' to describe how for years she had wandered through life thinking everybody else was living in paradise and that she would never experience it. My heart broke as I listened to her talk about the amazing turn around in her life; she now knows that she had tasted paradise because of the drugs that now controlled her mental health issues, because of her husband and her friends and through the love of a God who had never left her. I think Nicky knows that whatever has happened in her life; breakdown, depression, voices in her head, hospitalisation, suicide attempts - nothing can separate her from the love of God.

Our chapter title come from the letter to the Romans which is one of the letters that the scholars are pretty sure was written by Paul and not one of his followers. It is a theological treatise and we have to get into the mind of Paul in order to understand it.

As far as we know Paul was born sometime between the years one and ten in Asia Minor in the Diaspora. The Diaspora is the way in which the Jewish people spread throughout the world because of exile and enslavement. The Jews created Synagogue worship in the places where they remained because they could not go to the temple in Jerusalem. Many young boys were sent to Jerusalem to study under the rabbi Gamaliel and learn the law. Paul went to Jerusalem to become a Rabbi and was a Pharisee, such a passionate one that he persecuted those Jews who said that Jesus is the Messiah.

His conversion is extraordinary and vital in understanding him. Paul journeys towards Damascus to flush out more Christians. He met the risen Jesus and realised that, in the name of religion, he had become a murderer. In the name of love he had become hate. It is a reminder to us that that which makes us holy can also make us evil if we use it to form God in our image and likeness and to protect ourselves against transformation. Religion is not always the gift that we think it is.

It seems to me that the real revolution that has to take place within us is in our understanding of who God is. False images of God can make us self-righteous and judgemental because we have made God out to be an extension of ourselves frowning on people who do not fit in with our narrow, moralistic attitude to life.

When you discover the sort of God who wants nothing from you in return for loving you, then you are on the road to conversion. That is what Paul discovered and what will lead to the letter to the Romans. Real conversion changes the way you see things and do things; it turns the world upside down and that is what happens to Paul. Do we see things in a totally different way because of our experience of Christ, or do we simply believe what everyone else believes but shroud it in religious language?

The scholars tell us that Paul wrote his letter to the Romans in Corinth, and that it was probably dated around the year 60. The letter was sent mainly to Gentile Christians and the letter first of all serves as an introduction to a community who did not know him personally. He uses the letter to draw together some of his thinking, and what you find primarily is that Paul knows God is love and that love underpins everything; and so we know the truth that nothing can separate us from that love.

Paul begins his letter with a traditional greeting to the Church in Rome and then adds six verses that describe the Good News that he says he preaches everywhere. This Good News is about Jesus who is both a descendant of David and God's Son, proved by God raising Jesus from the dead. It is about the love that has always been in the heart of God for humanity. That is the Good News. Paul then declares that God appointed him to preach this Good News so that everyone might have the opportunity to respond to the Jesus way. It is his way of making sure that the Roman Church understands what his mission is about. He continues with a prayer of thanksgiving for the growth that the Roman Christians are making in their faith and says that he wants to come and visit them.

Paul wants to make very clear the letter's main thrust. This Good News about Jesus is God's saving action for the world. Love is what saves us. No one is cursed by the law anymore. Jesus has shown us the heart of God; compassion, mercy, love flowing out towards us, made flesh in the body of Jesus so that we can look and say, 'that is who you are. You are the God who transforms the messiness of human life through the power of love.' All it takes is that we trust and believe in it. That means faith is central; everything starts and ends with it. Yet we do not really have faith in God's love and the power of that love to save us.

We think it is about what we do and how good we are. What Paul is trying to do is to turn that on its head and help us realise that life in its fulness is about the Goodness of God and not about our pathetic attempts to be worthy. The twelve step processes understand it. These are processes that help people deal with addictions and they encourage participants to hand their lives over to a higher power. It is faith in God that makes real God's saving power in our lives.

The first three chapters of the letter show that our lack of belief in God's love means that we are trapped, lost, a mess. Paul wants us to face the reality that we live in, and he paints a rather gloomy picture of existence without Christ. One of the truths that I have come to realise is that so many of us create an illusory world that we base our lives on. We would do anything rather than face our own need and poverty, anything than face the truth that we are not in control and that we are vulnerable and broken and weak. When we realise it, and somehow hand it over to God, then our weakness becomes our greatest strength.

We are not very good at being real, or at admitting our frailty. We wear masks and pretend to be something we are not. We live shallow, protected lives that are not honest, and Paul wants us to face reality; and it hurts. We do not want to face the truth of our weakness and our inability to do it by ourselves, but until we do, we will not begin to understand the strength of God's love to save us. Paul wants to make us feel desperate and needy. He is trying to make us long for salvation. If we do not long to be saved, then we will not experience salvation or see that there is a way out of the mess that we are in.

Psychologists tell us that deep within, all of us are either guilt based or shame based people; we carry the guilt of not being Good enough. We have a deep sense of shame about who we are. Most of us live life hating ourselves and rejecting that within us that we see as weak or immoral or bad. Obviously when we do that to ourselves, we do it to other people.

The problem is that we will not believe who we are, God's beloved children. I think most of the journey in faith is about discovering who we truly are. In these first chapters of Romans, Paul is not trying to tell us that we are bad people, but that we are needy people who need to know the truth of who we are. We have to discover that God really does love us, that we are children of God despite what has happened in our lives. That is our true identity. Guilt and shame will not help us know that. Only Jesus can do that. Thank God that is what Jesus has done.

It is when we realise that we are God's beloved son or daughter that life takes on a new meaning, and we know that God will never abandon us and that love is all around us and within us. It is then that we begin to realise that there is a better road to go on, a more fulfilling journey that will bring us life. It is then that we have the courage to live in the moment, not beset by worries about the future or plagued by the guilt of the past. It is then that we are able to hold everything lightly save for the love of a God who has given everything. It is then that we are free to give ourselves away for the sake of others.

For Paul, we do not come to God by always avoiding sin. As a Church we seem to have spent so much time trying to turn people into Good Christians by showing them how to avoid sin. Paul tells us the truth that we come to God by recognising that we are trapped in sin, and by understanding how empty and stupid it is. The very struggle with sin becomes our salvation. We come to God, not by getting things right, but by getting things wrong, Paul knows that. We have to know we are trapped and that God is the only way out, otherwise we do not need God. It is why in the Easter Exultet we sing, 'O happy fault, O necessary sin of Adam.'

The concluding verses of this section summarise the point of the entire discussion since chapter 1. In the presence of God, no one is free from sin; and so somehow God has to deal with it in a way that we will understand. The Good News for Paul is that God has dealt with it all in Jesus, the visible manifestation of who God has always been, and all we have to do is realise it. Nothing can separate us from the love of God.

Chapters 5 to 8:39 is all about the Christian life, but it is not muscular Christianity: gritting your teeth and making sure that you love everyone without exception. It is a life that is based on responding to God's love. It is about becoming love for the world and allowing the power of love that you've received to flow through you.

Paul also talks about freedom from sin and death, freedom from self and the freedom to serve. It is very clear from what we have talked about that he sees freedom from sin and death as being God's initiative and he reflects on it drawing a parallel between Adam and Jesus. Adam is a 'type' or 'prototype' of the person to come, namely Jesus, who would far surpass what Adam did. Adam unleashed an active, hostile force into the world which we call sin, which damages our relationship with God because it makes us forget who we are in God's sight. It blinds our eyes to love; it stops us seeing. Jesus effect is completely different.

What Adam destroyed Jesus restores; humanity has the possibility of seeing and knowing who we really are in God's sight because of all that Jesus has done. Again it is all about faith, trusting, believing and responding to that love. Paul sees baptism as key in responding to love

Paul cannot understand how anyone could think of returning to a way of life where we do not know our own dignity or value or worth. How can anybody deny this 'really real', as Richard Rohr calls it and return to a way of life that traps us and binds us up? For Paul, it is simply unthinkable which is why he writes, 'In the same way you must see yourself as being dead to sin but alive for God in Christ Jesus.'

Having discussed freedom, Paul now finishes his discussion with another explanation of how believers are freed from the Jewish law. He points out that the 'law' stands for religious observance as a way of salvation. It involves a legalistic approach to life which does not give us the energy to fulfil it. In other words, Paul is saying, stop trying to fulfil the law by yourself, in your own power, and let the Spirit of love enable you to respond to God. I often think our churches are full of people trying to do it in their own power, who see legalism as the only way to be at peace with God, and who live frightened of their own shadow. It is love that matters and which frees us.

In chapter 8: 1 39, Paul reflects on life in the Spirit. The wonderful passage at the end of Romans 8 is the climax of the epistle at this point. The whole chapter answers the question in 7:24, 'Who will deliver me from this body doomed to death?' The liberator is the Spirit which is the power or force of the risen Jesus present upon earth. We are living in the Spirit when we are willing to trust in Jesus and in what he has done. This Spirit brings a vitality that the Mosaic law never could.

In verse 4 of chapter 8, Paul talks of the flesh and the Spirit. I have written about this before but I think it is worth reminding ourselves of what he means if we are really going to understand God's love for us. Most of us think that Spirit is Good, and flesh is bad. Our minds immediately tell us, because of our teaching, that Spirit has to do with God and flesh has to do with the body. Paul does not mean that at all. The issue is between the false self and the true self. The false self can be recognised in our control needs. It is characterised by seeing my desires and wants and needs as being of principal value. The true self or Spirit is who you really are in God. It is the knowledge that you are a child of God, and that is the only reality that matters. This knowledge is pure gift and has nothing to do with being a pious, church-going, religious person. It is an overwhelming from God, it is something which is given to us, it comes from outside, it is beyond our control but when we receive it we know it is our deepest self. The one who receives this gift of the Spirit finally feels whole.

The contrast between Spirit and flesh which is introduced in verse 4 is further developed in verses 5 13. Those who live in the false self lead a life that is less than is in the heart of God for them. The person living in the Spirit finds both life and peace;

they know who they are in the sight of God and know the relationship they have with God who is Abba Father.

The end of chapter 8 is a hymn of celebration of the reality of being in the Spirit. God is for us, and Paul wants us to know there is nothing, absolutely nothing, that can separate us from the love of God made visible in Christ Jesus our Lord. Nothing! Do you really hear that word nothing? We allow the mess of our own lives to get in the way and presume that because we do not like ourselves, God could not possibly like or love us. However Paul says no reality can ever separate us from the love of God, absolutely nothing, no pattern of behaviour, no moral short-comings, no state of being, nothing can separate us from the love of God. Those who live their lives trusting in the freedom that comes from Christ are beginning to know just that. Paul continues to explore this until, in 11:33-36, he ends with a brief but marvellous hymn of praise to the all merciful God. Paul has no doubt that God understands what history and human life are about, and that somehow God's purposes will be fulfilled; but it is never in the way we expect, and always through the loving power of God in which we both die and rise to new life.

In Romans 12:1 15:13, we find Paul reflecting on the invitation that believers are given to live life to the full, not as a response to law but as a response to the love of God which is poured out upon us. Everything is a response to love. We do not have to do things in our own strength, but in the strength of love which is all around us if we would only open our eyes and see it. We are chosen to understand what life is really about. We are set apart to influence the world by the way we live, and to somehow show the world what it means to really be human and alive; and not to do that is to live at a superficial level only enjoying a percentage of what God has created us for.

My friend Jackie is just such a person. Retired now, he lives very quietly with his wife and children; but throughout his life he has always been aware of the love of God. His conscious awareness of that love has led him to realise that materialism, wealth and competition are not the way to live life to the full. He has listened and responded to the Spirit within himself, and the power of love has become his guiding force. His is a very simple way of life based on the Gospel value of love above everything. That awareness has led him to a deep level of perception of what it means to be human and alive. Because of his wisdom, many people have beaten a pathway to his door, to sit and listen and be supported in their own quest to find life in its fulness. This wonderful, deep, richly human man has found a peace that surpasses all understanding and shares it with others.

It is obvious from all Paul's writings that he is profoundly influenced by his theology of 'body'. We are the body of Christ, and as body, we should promote a life of peace and harmony among all believers. Individuals should strengthen one another and encourage one another to fulfil their potential and become fully part of the body.

So in the final part of Romans, Paul makes three appeals to the believers in Rome: they ought to offer themselves in living sacrifice to God; they ought to shape their culture, not reflect it; They ought to let God transform them through his Spirit. This is done by co-operating for the common Good. No one is to think more highly of themselves at the expense of others. Gifts are to be used for the Good of everyone, not to make people feel Good about themselves or to make some people appear better than others.

Faith is about vertical and horizontal relationship and one without the other is not faith. So Paul says that the one who preaches is to be faithful to the truth of a God who is love; the one who serves is to help people materially; some should encourage those who need encouragement.

Both Rome and Corinth were port cities which had many neglected widows and orphans, had a constant stream of workers coming to their harbours, and many poor and sick. He obviously wants to try and curb the over-emphasis on the gifts of the Spirit, to let people know that faith is more than that. So Paul encourages the Christians in Rome to meet the needs of those around them We probably need to hear this in our Church, where we like to do religious things but not get involved in the lives of one another

Having encouraged this attitude of reaching out, Paul then sets to on the inner attitudes that effect people; do not curse your enemies; have the same attitude toward everyone. In the words of Jesus, turn the other cheek. Paul then talks about duties toward civil authority and about duties to one another and wants to stress above all else the primacy and governance of love. This fulfils the law that is to be written in our hearts,

In chapter 14:1-12, Paul has only one overriding principle: mutual respect and acceptance. God has accepted each person. Can we do less? We cannot judge one another and yet we do it all the time. We jump to conclusions about people's motivation, about the reasons others do things or do not do things and often it is a way of avoiding the issue of facing ourselves. It is a smoke screen that means we do not have to change or be converted. In the rest of chapter 14:13-23, Paul tells us that his desire for all believers is peace, joy and justice. The love of God should cause all believers to live together in righteousness, in peaceful openness to all, and in a joy that comes from standing open handed in the presence of God. In everything Paul says we are to follow the example of Jesus, even if that means suffering persecution and misunderstanding. Love is to be our motivation and our guiding force

Then finally Paul appeals for unity. He urges mutual acceptance and understanding, and he tells the Romans how important it is that they are welcoming and loving towards those who come to faith in Jesus, even if they do not see things in quite the same way as we do. Again, it is a challenge never to reject people of other traditions because they see things differently than we do; never be separated by issues such as, the gay issue, or women's role and ministry. Never let it close dialogue or mutual acceptance of one another.

Writing this letter to the Romans, Paul wants his readers in Rome and those of us reading the letter centuries on to know the primacy of love; love that flows from the heart of God and which invades our lives and leads us to live lives of loving service.

Above everything he wants us to know that nothing can separate us from the love of God and once we know, then its truth will sustain us every day of our lives.

TWELVE

SENT OUT TO LOVE

I WAS VERY SAD RECENTLY TO HEAR OF THE DEATH OF SHEILA. I first got to know her through her husband Mike, who was my brother Paul's maths teacher. Mike was one of those teachers who both inspired and challenged, and he certainly had a profound influence on Paul's life. Sheila and Mike lived in our parish and because I knew who Mike I was, I got to know who Sheila was. I have to say, when I first met her, I was a bit frightened of her. She was very down to earth and had no nonsense about her. She said what she thought and was always up for a challenge; but she often had a smile on her face and her eyes usually sparkled with laughter and energy.

In 1977, my mum started a prayer group in our house, and I can remember the first meeting as though it was yesterday. More and more people arrived, until they were sitting on the floor in the lounge and standing in the hall. I was very surprised to see Sheila standing halfway down the hall. I am not sure she understood what was going on, but she did say to me, many years later, that something kept drawing her back. After a couple of months of meeting in the house, we moved into the monastery; which was not a good move. The priests and brothers, at the time, did not really want a prayer group in their house and made it very obvious. We eventually moved again, into what turned out to be the prayer group's 'forever home,' in the Good Shepherd convent in Liverpool. All through those days of turbulence, Sheila kept coming to the prayer group, but she would never do a life in the spirit seminar. For seven weeks each year, she stopped attending and then would come back again. Eventually she took courage and attended one, and when she was baptised in the spirit, it seemed as though the love of God exploded within her. Afterwards, she said that because of that experience, she found the strength to do what turned into her life's ministry. She began to work with the divorced and separated, and through the years did a huge amount of work, healing broken hearts and transforming lives. She told me that it was when she knew she was loved by God that she felt within her a pull to love those who were broken. Pretty soon after that experience, Sheila stopped coming to the prayer group, but she never stopped acknowledging how that explosion of love had brought her faith to life and led her more deeply into the ways of love.

Whenever I think about the love of Jesus, I am immediately drawn to the cross, and sometimes I have to stop myself from going there. It would be easy to focus on his death and all that means for us, but actually his death is a visual representation of his life, and his life was lived as an immense outpouring of love on the world. This was so we would know the face of God and see what God is like for us. It is almost as though God has said you will never really understand how much you are loved, so I will have to show you in a human body so that you can see touch, almost taste, my unconditional love for you. Pope Francis recently said, 'the first step that God takes toward us is that of a love that anticipates and is unconditional. God is the first to love.

God does not love because there is something in us that engenders love. God loves us because he himself is love and, by its very nature, love tends to spread and give itself. God does not even condition his benevolence on our conversion. If anything, this is a consequence of God's love.' These are powerful words about the unconditional nature of God's love. Certainly, I think knowing that we are loved implies that no matter how we are feeling, how well or sick we become, God's love is always available to us and is not beyond our reach, because it is a deeply personal experience. It lets us know the truth that we are beloved children of God and that we have dignity and esteem that we can never create by our own efforts. It is sheer gift.

A lot of the mystics and great saints seem to have an encounter with love. Many of them describe that God, because of love, as the prime mover of love, is the author and creator of love. This means that God is the one who initially calls us into love and pours love out upon us. I love the words of Catherine of Siena who heard God say, 'I can love you more than you can love yourself and I watch over you a thousand times more carefully than you can watch over yourself'; or the wonderful Julian of Norwich, who said of God, 'in his love he clothes us, enfolds and embraces us; that tender love completely surrounds us, never to leave us.'

When we have that sort of experience of love, we certainly want to love God back. We want to respond to love with love. Richard Rohr says, 'mystics experience a full-bodied embrace and acceptance by Divine Love, and then spend their lives trying to verbalise and embody it. They invariably find ways to give that love back through forms of service and worship, but it is never earning love, it is always returning the love.'

Yet for most Christians, it is extremely hard to accept that unconditional love. Most of us have been brought up to believe that we should love God, and yet the sort of God that was portrayed to many of us was a monster. Why would we love such a God; and certainly why would we believe that God loves us with an infinite tenderness and mercy?

God created us, and knows that to be loved is necessary for a healthy emotional life. Our emotionality helps us to experience loving relationships which give us life and joy. If those emotions are damaged or repressed in any way, then it becomes harder to cultivate good healthy relationships. Look at the number of people who are unable to have good relationships as adults because of what has happened to them as children. The same is true of our understanding of God's love. If we have been fed the lie that God is anything other than loving, we will find it terribly hard to relate to God in a healthy, life-giving way. Sadly, it is often our brokenness and our need for healing and trans-formation which get in the way of knowing God's unconditional love and mercy. It seems to me that any right reading of the scriptures will tell us that, no matter how chaotic our lives seem or what our past has been, the love of Christ never stops pursuing us, offering itself to us repeatedly. It is a bit like Francis Thompson's poem 'The Hound of Heaven,' which talks of the pursuit of a loving God for all human beings. God's love for us is not stagnant but full of life, energy and dynamism. As St. Augustine said, 'You have called to me, and have cried out and have shattered my deafness...You have sent forth fragrance, I have drawn in my breath, and I pant after you. I have tasted you and I hunger and thirst after you. You have touched me, and I have burned for your peace.'

After his baptism in the Jordan, Jesus knew in a more unique way than he had before that God loved him. He had within himself an awareness of that life, energy and dynamism. Because of that, he had a capacity to support, encourage and renew people's lives, relationships and faith. If you look at the Gospels, you will see that for Jesus people were of the utmost value and importance, and anything that stopped people knowing who they were in God's eyes had to be named for what it was; evil. If he, Jesus, was a child of God, loved and accepted by the Father, then, as far as he was concerned, others had to know that same truth deep within themselves. The desire of the heart of God is that we would know that love is at the centre of God's nature, and indeed, at the centre of the universe. Jesus, the human face of God, went to any lengths to show us that we are loved. We find him attacking the Scribes and the Pharisees, those who put burdens on the poor and the needy. He denounced contemporary religious practices which, instead of setting people free, bound them up even more tightly. We find him loving people into freedom through healing and forgiveness. The love of God in Jesus confronts, challenges and cuts through so much of the unnecessary trivia we surround ourselves with.

God's love is not always comfortable because it calls us to life and away from that which is illusion.

We discover, in Jesus, a God who sets people free from their pasts. Most of us judge people because of their pasts and do not allow them the luxury of changing. In John's Gospel, we have the beautiful stories of the woman taken in adultery, about to lose her life, and the Samaritan woman chained up by her past and her reputation. In Luke's Gospel we have the story of Zaccheus, the taxman whose encounter with Jesus led him to give away half of everything he owned. Nowhere did he judge those people or criticise them; and so they found the power to change. God's love is a present moment reality. Jesus shows us the God who allows us to be free from anything we have ever done. He accepted the marginalised and the outcast and because he mixed with them, he became one with them. He became one of the unclean. I think that statement is really hard for us to take on, but it is true. Generally, the Mosaic Law spoke of something as being unclean if it was unfit to use in worship to God. Being 'clean' or 'unclean' was a ceremonial label affecting the ritual of corporate worship. There were certain animals considered unclean and not to be used in sacrifices, and there were certain actions, like touching a dead body, which made the person who touched that body unclean and unable to participate in worship until they had been cleansed. Specific foods such as pork, certain fish, and certain birds were unclean for Jews and forbidden for them to eat. A skin infection could make a person unclean, or unfit for worship or even to be part of the community. A house with certain kinds of mould was unclean. A woman was unclean

for a period of time following childbirth. An animal offered for
sacrifice had to be without defect. The person who offered the
sacrifice also had to be 'clean' before the Law. The cure of the
woman with the haemorrhage, and the daughter of Jairus who
is raised to life in Luke's Gospel illustrate this so clearly. The
woman particularly is on her uppers. She is completely unclean.
Anyone who touches her is the same. It is a huge risk for her to
go into a crowd of people and yet she knows who can help her;
and what does Jesus do? He lets her touch him. As I have said,
in Jewish law to touch a dead body would make a person
unclean. Jesus goes right in and takes Jairus' daughter by the
hand. It is extraordinary love. Tax collectors, sinners, prostitutes,
all found a place with him, and his acceptance brought them
healing and peace. They found freedom. They knew through
him that they were loved and accepted, and nothing could take
that away from them. God reaches out to the broken and the
little ones with a compassion and mercy that we will never
understand unless we have been there. God is with us in
the mess. He gave people choices and options. I think that is
illustrated best by the story of the rich young man. At no point
did Jesus force anyone to do what he wanted; he simply, offered
and allowed, people the freedom to walk away and he still
loved them. Most of us try to manipulate others to get them to
do what we want, usually because of insecurity. God loves us so
much that he freely allows us to do what we choose to do.
He told story after story to try and illustrate a God who is
always reaching out to us. Think of the stories I mentioned in
the chapter 'parables of love.' The father who was constantly
looking out for the son who had wronged him so badly; the

shepherd who looks for the one sheep that is missing; or the woman whose searches for the coin that she has lost and then throws a party that probably cost more than the coin. Hear phrases like, 'You are worth more than hundreds of sparrows or 'how much more will God look after you than the lilies of the fields?

Jesus' life shows us the reality of God's love. Jesus' life shows us that God is concerned with what happens to us physically, materially and spiritually. Jesus' life shows us love. But the amazing reaction in the Gospel stories is that the vast majority of people do not respond; and so Jesus walks to Calvary not to appease an angry God, but to show us in a human body that God is always the eternal giver. It is as though each of the evangelists is saying you will finally understand who God is for us when you see the crucified Lord, when you see love poured out. Our God is the eternal giver and that eternal giving of God is made flesh in the crucified Jesus. There is nothing you can do that will stop God loving you, wanting you or desiring you. I hope you have heard throughout this book that God's love is not conditional. It is poured out constantly for us, and it hangs on the cross on the rubbish dump of Golgotha. Somehow in that giving, our sin, our brokenness, our pain is swallowed up and we are healed. We are submerged in the power of love. It is a bit like being in love with someone; you somehow do not see their sin and their brokenness, and if you do it does not matter. It is somehow swallowed up in the power of love and is no longer important.

If you had been the only person in the world God would still have become flesh in Jesus and love would have visited the earth. If you had been the only person in the world God would still have gone to Calvary for you. If you had been the only person in the world, God would still have hung on the cross for you so that you would know how much you are loved, so that you would know that your sin and your pain and your broken-ness is swallowed up in the love that knows no end. I always think it is so sad that we have made religion into something we do to get into another world. It is about living now, knowing the truth that you are loved by God, that you do not deserve it, that you cannot earn it, and that it is poured out for you constantly. It is about knowing the truth of the Lamb of God and the truth of God's sacrificial love that heals and transforms us; and it is therefore about allowing that love to propel you into loving others with the same love that Jesus showed.

There is the rub! As soon as we open ourselves to the power of God's love, we become aware of the needs of those around us and the call to love as Jesus loved. As the late, great theologian Karl Rahner wrote: 'Christians by their very nature are supposed to witness to the unfathomable reality that God loves us. They have to love in deeds and not just in convictions and words, for those near and those far away.' It is all summed up in John's Gospel when Jesus takes a towel and a bowl of water and washes his disciples' feet. Immediately after that, John has Jesus issue the challenge in one little phrase, 'I give you a new commandment: love one another. Just as I have loved you, you also should love one another.' If we know God's love, we are sent out to bring that love to others. The word command in the original Greek means an injunction, ordinance, or law. Jesus was not only calling us with an authoritative order, but he was also instituting a new law, the law of love, to replace the law of Moses. We are called to love one another, to walk in the new law of love. The command goes even further. When Jesus told his disciples to love one another, he said to do it 'as I have loved you.' That is a tall order. The word agape which John uses, means to love like God loves. We are commanded to love without thought of ourselves. We are literally to pour ourselves out for the sake of others. We are called to love wholeheartedly and sacrificially like God loves us.

If you go to Luke's Gospel and read the story of the good Samaritan, it becomes noticeably clear that the love which we are to share is for everyone who crosses our path. Jesus tells the story of the good Samaritan to answer a lawyer who asks the question of him, 'who is my neighbour.' The story basically says everyone is your neighbour regardless of who they are, where they have come from, what their colour is or their sexual orientation. It is a fantastic reflection on the core of the Gospel message as it reminds us that we are the ones who are to go the extra mile even when we are being taken for a ride. Just recently I was in Liverpool city centre, and I stopped to have a chat with a man sitting in an empty shop doorway. We did not chat for long but as I left him, I shook his hand, wished him well and dropped some money in his tin. As I walked away from him, a woman came up to me to tell me I was wasting my money and my time because under his blanket the man had hidden a can of cider. She went on to make it clear that he was conning me. I think she was a bit confused when I smiled at her and said that was fine and then turned around and dropped some more money in his can. The Gospel message of love is all about being willing to give without counting the cost and it demands, if we are taking it seriously, that we are the ones who stand with our brothers and sisters who find life difficult. Our main characteristics are that we are the ones who are not to judge and condemn the alcoholic and the addict and those on the edge of society. Sadly, and all too often, we are the ones who do exactly that, turning away from those in need and judging and condemning, often from a place of ignorance. About an hour after my encounter with the woman who told me I was being conned, I went to Mass in the Blessed Sacrament Shrine and there she was large as life in the front row. We can so easily be like the Priest and the Levite who see what is going on but pass by on the other side, and encourage others to do the same. We can be particularly good at quoting this doctrine or that doctrine and knowing all the rules of the Church. The Pharisees at the time of Jesus were like that. We can spend a fortune on going to pilgrimages here, there and everywhere; we can quote visionary after visionary but unless we are learning how to love then we have not even begun to understand what Jesus is about and our religious practice is empty. To walk in love is about loving your enemies, your neighbour, yourself, and anyone you come across who needs your love. I was reading recently that because God is love and we are made in God's image and likeness, the very fabric of our being requires that we both receive and share love. Maybe that is why Jesus gives us a new commandment.

In Matthew's Gospel, we hear Jesus spell out what love means in a practical sense when he says, 'love your enemies, do good to those who hurt you.' I think that most people within the Christian tradition, and indeed most major religions, would recognise the call to both love and forgive. Several years ago, Megan McKenna spoke at one of our conferences. During the session, she asked participants to talk with the person next to them about love and forgiveness. She then asked for feedback and one man said something like, 'well it is hard to do and after all we are only human.' Megan responded in her usual forthright way by reminding us that we are far more than just human; we have the spirit of God within us and so we can love and forgive, even our enemies. Yet most of us are like the man who responded to Megan's question. We see loving and forgiving our enemies as an ideal rather than as a practical reality. Some of us even think that we are doing it, until something happens in our lives and we find love and forgiveness hard to do. When writing about love and forgiveness, Ronald Rolheiser concludes, 'we really do not love and forgive those who oppose us. Too often we are distrustful, disrespectful, bitter, demonising, and (metaphorically speaking) murderous towards each other. If there is much love and forgiveness of enemies in our lives, it is far from evident, both in our world and in our churches.' What a sad indictment that is on us: that we have not really got to grips with a central truth of our faith, but, I think, concern ourselves with other truths that are arguably less important.

So the question is, how do we love and forgive as Jesus did?

Jesus often faced opposition. He often encountered people who were bitter and angry. He was misunderstood on many occasions and, in response, he never allowed his heart to become bitter or angry. He was always loving, forgiving, warm, accepting, kind, non-violent and, at times, mischievous. There were undoubtedly moments when his words were harsh to get his point across, but not because he wanted to hurt those who listened but because he wanted to give them an opportunity to change. Like all human beings, this way of loving and forgiving was probably the most challenging part of his life and mission. In order to live it out, he took himself apart to commune with God and to find the strength to love. Ronald Rolheiser has written, 'Jesus, it seems, set himself apart, not by externals, clothing and symbols, but through the integrity of his life. Where he showed himself to be different was by not sinning, by praying for whole nights, by fasting and going off by himself into the desert, by forgiving his enemies, by constant intimacy with God, and by being morally faithful when everyone else betrayed.' Should we be any different? So, because of love, we are impelled to love and in that loving, to transform the world that we have been given. One of my favourite quotations is from the El Salvadorian Saint Oscar Romero, who fought for the poor, and who was murdered by the El Salvadorian government while he was celebrating Mass on March 24th, 1980. I would like to finish this chapter with Romero's words which are all about transforming love:

This is what we are about.

We plant the seeds that one day will grow.

We water seeds already planted, knowing that they hold future promise.

We lay foundations that will need further development.

We provide yeast that produces far beyond our capabilities.

We cannot do everything, and there is a sense of liberation in realising that.

This enables us to do something, and to do it very well.

It may be incomplete, but it is a beginning, a step along the way, an opportunity for the Lord's grace to enter and do the rest.

We may never see the end results, but that is the difference between the master builder and the worker.

We are workers, not master builders; ministers, not messiahs.

We are prophets of a future not our own.

Oscar Romero

CONCLUSION

I TEACH A MODULE ON OUR LOCAL CATHOLIC CERTIFICATE IN Religious Studies course. It is a national initiative to try and help inform teachers in Catholic schools about the Catholic tradition. Occasionally, I have sat on trains reading the essays that students submit at the end of the module for assessment. Sometimes they are good but more often than not they are exasperating! One day I was tutting away at one of these essays and the man opposite me smiled and asked me what I was marking. I told him and he smiled more broadly and said, 'well, I guess from your response they are not great.' I laughed and said 'no.' He then started to talk. His name was Mark and, shamefacedly, he told me that he was a lapsed Catholic. It was because he had huge problems with the Bible when he was young and every time he asked a question he got into trouble and was beaten by the Christian brother that he asked. So he gave up asking and he gave up searching. I felt so sad and found myself apologising to him that no-one had taken his questions seriously and I directed him towards a couple of books that might help.

It seems to me that the Scriptures answer the questions so many people are asking as they search for truth about themselves, about love and about God. All the time we are being invited to move deeper in understanding love, God and self. Because of the progressive revelation of God, they remind us that there is always more, and that however much we discover each day there is newness and freshness. It does not matter how old you are, or how young you are, there is more.

One of the Greek words that John uses in his Gospel is the word psyche, which means the centre of a person's life. It is the place where we feel our human emotions and desires and where we can begin to discover God. The whole of the Bible is leading us to know that if we enter into the deepest part of ourselves, that part that defies expression, we will discover God. It is wonderful. God lives within us, and we will discover God's presence if we are prepared to journey, struggle and not stay at the superficial level of life that so many of us live at, reducing life to a list of moral expectations and faith to a pile of religious practices that help no one.

The Scriptures will lead us into love if we let them. They will help us experience the love that breathed the world and the universe into being and which holds it together. They will lead us into the love that underpins everything and which was made flesh in Jesus.

Somehow, in Jesus, we come to know the source of everything that exists and the end to which everything is moving; but more than that, the good news is that this power of love is Father, with all that means and this power of love is calling us to become what God intended: people who live life to the full and experience that love. In a sense, what happens is that we find in this love the reality of ourselves.

This book has been an attempt to add to the journey into love. I hope it has laid to rest some of fears that we might have had and given some a new impetus to this journey into God. So if you have read this book, fully or partial, or even if you just liked the title or someone gave it to you as a gift, I would encourage you to go on the journey. Search and discover and you will know what real life is about.

Further copies of this book
and other books by Fr Chris Thomas

Love is the Key
When Did we Stop Skipping?
Meta... What?
Holiness is for Everyone
Forgiveness is for Giving
Let it Begin with Me
Give Thanks With a Grateful Heart
Who Do You Say I Am?
O God, You Search Me and You Know Me
Blessed Are You

are available from:

Goodnews Books
Upper Level
St. John's Church
296 Sundon Park Road
Luton, Beds. LU3 3AL

01582 571011
www.goodnewsbooks.co.uk
orders@goodnewsbooks.co.uk